RETIREMENT PLANNING FOR BEGINNERS

RETIREMENT PLANNING FOR BEGINNERS

A COMPREHENSIVE GUIDE TO BUILDING SAVINGS,
MAXIMIZING INCOME, AND ACHIEVING
FINANCIAL SECURITY FOR YOUR GOLDEN YEARS

FINANCIAL PLANNING ESSENTIALS
BOOK 1

CALVIN BOSWELL

B
Book Bound
STUDIOS

To all who stand at the threshold of tomorrow, may this guide illuminate your path to a future filled with security, fulfillment, and the joy of well-earned rest. Here's to building dreams that last a lifetime.

The best time to plant a tree was 20 years ago. The second best time is now.

— CHINESE PROVERB

CONTENTS

EMBARKING ON YOUR RETIREMENT JOURNEY

Understanding the Importance of Retirement Planning

Embarking on the retirement planning journey is akin to setting sail on a vast ocean. The waters may be uncharted and the horizon distant. Still, with a sturdy vessel and a reliable compass, the journey can lead to a destination of comfort and security in your later years. Understanding the importance of retirement planning is the first step in charting your course to a fulfilling retirement.

Retirement planning is essential because it is about more than just ensuring you have enough money to live on after you stop working. It's about crafting a vision for your life that extends beyond your career. This vision encompasses financial stability and considers how you will spend your time, where you will live, and what activities will fill your days. You may be adrift without a plan, subject to economic change and personal circumstances.

The importance of retirement planning cannot be overstated. It's a process that allows you to take control of your financial future and provides peace of mind that you can maintain your standard of living when you are no longer earning a regular income. It's about ensuring that your golden years are just that—golden.

Moreover, retirement planning is not a one-size-fits-all endeavour. It requires a personalized approach that considers your unique financial situation, goals, and risk tolerance. It's about understanding how much you need to save, how to invest your savings to keep pace with or outpace inflation, and how to protect your nest egg from potential financial pitfalls.

One of the most critical aspects of retirement planning is starting early. The power of compounding interest means that the sooner you begin saving, the more time your money has to grow. Even small amounts saved regularly can accumulate into significant sums over time. Conversely, delaying your savings plan can require you to save much more aggressively later in life, which may not be as feasible or could lead to a less comfortable retirement.

In addition to saving, effective retirement planning involves managing debt, understanding your retirement income sources such as Social Security and pensions, and considering the impact of taxes on your retirement savings. It also means being prepared for unexpected expenses and understanding the healthcare costs in retirement.

As you embark on this journey, remember that retirement planning is not static. It is dynamic and should be revisited regularly to adjust for life changes, economic fluctuations, and shifts in your goals and circumstances. It's about building a flexible plan to weather the storms and take advantage of favorable winds, guiding you safely to the shores of a well-deserved and well-planned retirement.

You are better equipped to move forward with a clear understanding of why retirement planning is so crucial. The next step in your journey is to set realistic retirement goals that align with your vision and provide a tangible destination for your planning efforts.

Setting Realistic Retirement Goals

As we embark on the retirement journey, setting realistic retirement goals is the compass that will guide us through the uncharted waters of our future. It's about aligning our aspirations with our financial capabilities, ensuring the golden years are as golden as we envision them.

To begin with, let's consider what retirement means to you personally. Is it a time for relaxation and leisure, a period to explore new hobbies, or an opportunity to travel the world? It's an opportunity to volunteer and give back to the community or even to start a small business. Your retirement goals should reflect your deepest desires for this significant phase of life.

Once you've painted a picture of your ideal retirement, it's time to ground those dreams in reality. Start by assessing your current financial situation. How much have you already saved? What are your expected sources of income in retirement? These include social security benefits, pensions, investments, or part-time work.

Next, estimate the cost of your retirement dreams. If travel is a priority, research and calculate the expenses associated with your dream destinations. If you hope to relocate, consider the cost of living in the new area. Don't forget to factor in the everyday expenses—housing, food, healthcare, and insurance—that will continue into retirement.

Inflation is a silent factor that can erode your purchasing power over time. When setting your retirement goals, account for the possibility that life will cost more down the line. A general rule of thumb is to plan for an annual inflation rate of 2-3%, adjusting your savings goals accordingly.

Longevity is another critical factor. With advances in healthcare, many of us are living longer, which means we need our retirement savings to stretch further. Planning for a longer retirement ensures that you will retain your resources.

Once you've considered these factors, it's time to set specific, measurable, achievable, relevant, and time-bound (SMART) goals. For instance, instead of saying, "I want to have enough to retire comfortably," quantify what "comfortably" means to you. A SMART goal might be, "I aim to save $500,000 by the age of 65, which will allow me to withdraw $20,000 annually for 25 years in retirement."

Remember, your retirement goals aren't set in stone. Life's circumstances change, and you must review and adjust your goals periodically. A job change, an unexpected expense, or a shift in family dynamics can all impact your retirement planning. Regular check-ins on your financial progress will help you stay on track and make necessary adjustments.

In setting realistic retirement goals, you're not just dreaming about the future but actively constructing it. With each goal you set and each step you take towards it, you're building the foundation for a retirement that is as fulfilling as your working years.

The Basics of Retirement Income

Understanding the basics of retirement income is crucial. After setting your retirement goals, it's time to delve into the various sources of income that will support you during your golden years. This foundation will help you assess your financial health in the next planning stage.

Retirement income typically comes from three primary sources: **government pensions**, **employer-sponsored retirement plans**, and **personal savings and investments**. Each of these plays a different role in your overall retirement strategy.

Firstly, government pensions, such as Social Security in the United States, provide a foundational income covering many retirees' basic living expenses. The amount you receive is based on your earnings history and the age at which you choose to start receiving benefits. Understanding how these benefits work and what you can expect to receive is essential, as they will likely form the bedrock of your retirement income.

Secondly, employer-sponsored retirement plans, like 401(k)s or pension plans, are also significant. Suppose you have a 401(k). In that case, you've been contributing a portion of your income to this tax-advantaged account, often matched by employer contributions. On the other hand, pensions provide a fixed retirement income determined by your salary and years of service. Understanding the details of your employer-sponsored plan, including when you can access the funds and how they will be taxed, is essential for planning.

Lastly, personal savings and investments fill the gaps and provide additional income. This category includes savings accounts, individual retirement accounts (IRAs), stocks, bonds, and other investment vehicles. The income from these sources depends on the amount you've saved and how you've invested it. Managing your savings effectively involves understanding investment principles, risk tolerance, and the importance of diversification.

Remember, each of these income streams comes with its own set of rules, tax implications, and benefits. Understanding how they all fit together is essential to creating a stable and reliable income throughout your retirement.

Remember that your retirement income plan should be dynamic as you consider these income sources. It will likely change over time as your needs evolve and as you transition through different phases of retirement. Regular reviews and adjustments to your plan will help ensure that your retirement income remains aligned with your living expenses and lifestyle choices.

With a clear understanding of the basics of retirement income, you're better equipped to assess your current financial health, which is the next critical step in your retirement planning process. By evaluating your financial situation, you'll be able to identify any gaps between your expected income and your desired retirement lifestyle and make informed decisions to bridge those gaps.

Assessing Your Current Financial Health

As you stand at the threshold of your retirement journey, you must take a comprehensive look at your financial health. This assessment is not just about how much you have in your savings account; it's a holistic review of your financial landscape. Think of it as a personal balance sheet that will help you understand where you stand and what you need to do to reach your retirement goals.

To begin, let's focus on your assets. These are what you own that can be converted into cash. This includes checking and savings accounts, retirement accounts like 401(k)s and IRAs, and other investments such as stocks, bonds, mutual funds, and real estate. It's essential to get a clear picture of these resources because they will form the backbone of your retirement funding.

Next, consider your liabilities, which are your debts and obligations. This includes your mortgage, car loans, credit card debt, and other loans. Knowing what you owe is just as important as knowing what you own because these will affect your retirement savings and spending.

Once you clearly understand your assets and liabilities, it's time to calculate your net worth. Subtract your total liabilities from your total assets. This figure is a snapshot of your financial health and a starting point for retirement planning.

Now, let's delve into your income and expenses. Begin by listing all sources of income, including your salary if you're still working, rental income, dividends, and any other regular cash inflows. Then, track your expenses. It's crucial to be thorough here; account for everything from your daily coffee to your monthly mortgage payment. Understanding your cash flow is vital because it influences how much you can allocate towards retirement savings.

It's also important to consider the impact of inflation on your retirement savings. The cost of living will likely increase, and your retirement income needs to keep pace. Factor in a reasonable estimate for inflation as you plan for future expenses.

Lastly, review your insurance coverage, including health, life, and long-term care insurance. These policies protect your finances from unexpected events that could otherwise derail your retirement plans.

You're laying the groundwork for a successful retirement by assessing your current financial health. It's a process that requires honesty, thoroughness, and, sometimes, tough decisions. But remember, this is just the beginning. With a clear understanding of where you stand today, you'll be better equipped to map out the journey ahead and make the necessary adjustments to ensure your retirement is as comfortable and secure as possible.

Creating a Retirement Timeline

Having taken a clear look at your financial health, you're now ready to chart the course ahead. Creating a retirement timeline is much like mapping a long-awaited road trip; it requires understanding the starting point, destination, and milestones along the way. This section will guide you through the process of establishing a realistic and flexible timeline for your retirement.

Begin by envisioning your ideal retirement age. This is not just a number but a reflection of your career aspirations, health considerations, and personal goals. Do you see yourself retiring early to pursue hobbies or spend time with family? Or do you wish to extend your career as long as possible for personal fulfillment or financial reasons? Your target retirement age sets the stage for your planning.

Next, estimate your retirement lifespan. With advancements in healthcare, many retirees can expect to live 20 to 30 years or more post-retirement. Planning for longevity is crucial to avoid outliving your resources. Consider your family health history and lifestyle as you make this estimate, and err on the side of caution.

Break down your retirement into phases, as financial needs can change significantly over time. The early years may involve active spending on travel and hobbies, while later years might see increased healthcare costs. Understanding these phases helps in anticipating changes in cash flow needs.

With these considerations in mind, you can begin to outline your retirement timeline. Start from your current age and plot the significant financial events leading up to and through retirement. These events include paying off your mortgage, your children's graduation from college, significant birthdays, and your last day of work.

As you create this timeline, consider the financial milestones you'll need to hit to retire comfortably. These include the savings you'll need by certain ages, when to start shifting your investment strategy from growth to income, and when to begin taking Social Security benefits. Remember, these milestones should be treated as guideposts, not immovable markers. Life is unpredictable, and your timeline should allow for adjustments as circumstances change.

Finally, review your timeline regularly. Your retirement goals and financial situation will evolve as you progress through your career and personal life. An annual timeline review will help you stay on track and make necessary adjustments to account for changes in the economy, income, and personal life.

By creating a retirement timeline, you're not just planning for an event in the distant future; you're taking active steps to ensure your golden years are as secure and enjoyable as possible. With a clear path, you can proceed confidently, knowing that each step you take brings you closer to the retirement you envision.

BUILDING YOUR RETIREMENT SAVINGS

Introduction to Retirement Accounts

As you embark on the journey of retirement planning, one of the first and most crucial steps is understanding the various retirement accounts available to you. These accounts are not just places to stash your money until you're ready to leave the workforce; they are dynamic tools designed to grow your savings through tax advantages and investment opportunities.

A retirement account is a financial plan that allows you to set aside funds for your golden years. The beauty of these accounts lies in their preferential tax treatment, which helps your savings to grow more efficiently than they might in a standard savings account. There are several types of retirement accounts, and while they all serve the same general purpose, they differ in contribution limits, tax implications, and withdrawal rules.

The most common types of retirement accounts include Individual Retirement Accounts (IRAs), 401(k)s, and Roth IRAs. Traditional IRAs and 401(k)s offer tax-deferred growth whereas Roth IRAs are funded with after-tax dollars—however, more on these later. Employer-sponsored plans like 401(k)s are also pivotal in retirement planning—but, again, more on these later.

As you consider which retirement accounts to use, consider your current financial situation, tax bracket, retirement goals, and how you want to manage your taxes now versus in retirement. The choices you make can have a significant impact on the amount of money you will have available when you decide to retire.

Remember, the earlier you start contributing to these accounts, the more time your money has to grow. Even small, regular contributions can add up over time, thanks to the power of compound interest, which we will explore in the next section. By understanding the types of retirement accounts and starting to contribute to them, you're taking a vital step toward building a secure and comfortable retirement.

The Power of Compound Interest

Imagine a snowball rolling down a snowy hillside. As it rolls, it picks up more snow, growing larger and gaining momentum with every turn. This snowball effect is a perfect metaphor for compound interest, one of the most powerful forces in building retirement savings.

Compound interest occurs when the interest earned on your savings is reinvested to earn additional interest. It's interest on interest; over time, it can turn modest savings into a substantial nest egg. To harness the power of compound interest, you need to understand two key factors: the rate of return and time.

The rate of return is the percentage by which your investment grows each year. Even a tiny difference in this rate can significantly impact your savings. For example, a $10,000 investment with a 5% annual return will grow to about $26,500 in 20 years. Increase that return to 7%; the same investment swells to nearly $39,000. That's the power of a higher rate of return.

Time is the secret ingredient that makes compound interest genuinely magical. The longer your money is invested, the more time compound interest has to work wonders. This is why starting early can make such a profound difference. If you begin saving at age 25 rather than 35, those extra ten years could mean the difference between a comfortable retirement and a financially stressful one.

Let's illustrate this with an example. Two friends, Alex and Jordan, decided to save for retirement. Alex starts at age 25, contributing $3,000 annually to a retirement account with a 7% average annual return. By age 65, Alex will have contributed $120,000, but the investment will have grown to over $600,000 thanks to compound interest.

On the other hand, Jordan waits until age 35 to start saving the same amount each year under the same conditions. By age 65, Jordan will have contributed $90,000, but the account will have grown to only about $300,000. The ten-year delay cost Jordan a significant amount in potential earnings.

To make the most of compound interest, consider these practical steps:

1. **Start Early:** The sooner you begin saving, the more time compound interest has to grow your retirement savings.
2. **Save Regularly:** Consistent contributions, even negligible, can lead to significant growth over time.
3. **Reinvest Returns:** Ensure that the interest and dividends from your investments are reinvested to benefit from compounding.
4. **Be Patient:** Compound interest is a long-term strategy. Resist the temptation to dip into your savings, as this disrupts the compounding process.

Understanding and leveraging the power of compound interest is a cornerstone of retirement planning. It's a simple concept with profound implications: save early and often, and let time and the relentless force of compounding do the heavy lifting for your retirement savings.

As you consider the impact of compound interest on your retirement planning, you must make informed decisions about the types of retirement accounts you choose. Whether Roth or traditional, each account type has tax implications and growth potential, affecting how your investments compound over time. But that's another topic where we'll delve into the nuances of choosing the proper retirement account for your financial situation.

Choosing Between Roth and Traditional Accounts

As you build your retirement savings, one of the critical decisions you'll face is choosing between Roth and traditional retirement accounts. Both options offer unique benefits and can be powerful tools in your retirement planning arsenal. Understanding their differences is crucial to making an informed decision that aligns with your financial goals and circumstances.

Let's start with traditional retirement accounts, such as a

traditional IRA or a 401(k). The primary advantage of these accounts is that contributions are made with pre-tax dollars, which means you can deduct them from your taxable income in the year you make them. This upfront tax break can be particularly beneficial if you're in a higher tax bracket and expect a lower one during retirement. The money in a traditional account grows tax-deferred, meaning you will only pay taxes on the gains once you withdraw the funds in retirement. However, those withdrawals are taxed as ordinary income once you start taking distributions.

Conversely, Roth accounts offer a different tax advantage, like a Roth IRA or a Roth 401(k). Contributions to Roth accounts are made with after-tax dollars, so there's no immediate tax deduction. The trade-off, however, is that the withdrawals you make in retirement are completely tax-free, provided certain conditions are met. This includes the growth of your investments, which can be a significant benefit if you expect to be in the same or a higher tax bracket when you retire. Additionally, Roth accounts do not require you to take mandatory distributions after reaching a certain age, which is a requirement for traditional accounts.

When deciding between a Roth and a traditional account, consider your current income, expected future income, tax rates, and how long you have until retirement. If you anticipate that your retirement tax rate will be lower than it is now, a traditional account might make more sense. Conversely, a Roth account could be the better choice if you expect your tax rate to be higher in retirement or prefer the certainty of tax-free withdrawals.

It's also worth noting that you don't necessarily have to choose one. Many opt to have both accounts to diversify their tax exposure. This strategy can provide flexibility when it comes to planning and taking distributions in retirement.

Remember, the decision between Roth and traditional accounts is not set in stone. As your financial situation changes, it is beneficial to reevaluate your choice. The key is to start saving early, understand the tax implications, and adjust your strategy to maximize your retirement savings potential.

As you continue to explore your retirement planning options, it's essential to consider the role that employer-sponsored retirement plans can play in your overall strategy. These plans often come with additional benefits, such as employer matching contributions, which can significantly enhance your retirement savings efforts.

Employer-Sponsored Retirement Plans

When building your retirement savings, one of the most valuable resources at your disposal may be your employer-sponsored retirement plan. These plans, often referred to as 401(k)s, 403(b)s, or similar titles depending on your workplace, are not just a perk of your job—they are a cornerstone of modern retirement planning.

Employer-sponsored retirement plans offer a unique combination of benefits that can significantly enhance your ability to save for retirement. One of the most compelling features is the potential for employer-matching contributions. Many employers will match a portion of the money you contribute to your plan up to a certain percentage of your salary. This is free money, boosting your savings rate and helping your retirement fund grow more rapidly.

Another advantage of these plans is the high contribution limit. For 2023, the IRS allows you to contribute up to $20,500 to your 401(k) or similar plan, with an additional catch-up contribution of $6,500 if you are 50 or older. This limit is significantly higher than that of Individual Retirement Accounts (IRAs), which we will discuss later, allowing you to save more on a tax-advantaged basis.

The tax treatment of employer-sponsored plans is also a significant draw. Depending on whether you choose a traditional or Roth option within your plan—assuming your employer offers both—your contributions can either reduce your taxable income now or provide tax-free income in retirement. Traditional contributions are made pre-tax, lowering taxable income and providing tax-deferred growth. In contrast, Roth contributions are made with after-tax dollars, offering tax-free withdrawals in retirement.

It's important to note that the funds in these plans are typically invested in a selection of mutual funds, stocks, bonds, or other investment vehicles. Your plan may offer a range of investment options, each with different levels of risk and potential return. As a beginner, it's crucial to understand your own risk tolerance and investment horizon, as these will guide your selection of investments within the plan.

Enrolling in your employer's retirement plan is usually straightforward. Most employers provide an enrollment period when you first join the company; some may automatically enroll you in the plan. If you need help getting started, your human resources department can guide you on the enrollment process and the options available to you.

Once you're enrolled, managing your contributions is critical. If possible, aim to contribute at least enough to get the full employer match; not doing so would mean leaving valuable retirement dollars on the table. Over time, as your financial situation allows, consider increasing your contributions to maximize your savings potential.

In summary, employer-sponsored retirement plans are a powerful tool in your retirement savings arsenal. They offer generous contribution limits, potential employer matching, and favorable tax treatment. By taking full advantage of these plans, you can build a solid foundation for your retirement savings, setting the stage for a more secure financial future.

While employer-sponsored plans are a significant part of retirement savings, they are not the only option. It's also essential to understand the role of Individual Retirement Accounts, or IRAs, which offer additional opportunities to save for retirement with tax advantages. We'll explore the basics and benefits of IRAs in our continued discussion on building a robust retirement savings strategy.

Chapter Summary

- Retirement accounts are designed to grow savings through tax advantages and investment opportunities, with different types offering varying contribution limits and tax implications.
- Common retirement accounts include Traditional IRAs, 401(k)s, and Roth IRAs, each with unique tax benefits and rules for contributions and withdrawals.
- Early contributions to retirement accounts are crucial due to the power of compound interest, which allows savings to grow exponentially over time.
- The rate of return and the length of time money is invested are critical factors in maximizing the benefits of compound interest.
- Choosing between Roth and traditional retirement accounts depends on one's current and expected future tax rates, with Roth accounts offering tax-free withdrawals in retirement.
- Employer-sponsored retirement plans, such as 401(k)s, often include employer matching contributions and have higher contribution limits than IRAs, providing significant retirement savings opportunities.
- Contributions to employer-sponsored plans can be made pre-tax for traditional options or after-tax for Roth options, affecting taxable income and retirement withdrawals.

- Individual Retirement Accounts (IRAs) offer additional opportunities to save for retirement with tax advantages, complementing employer-sponsored plans in a retirement savings strategy.

INVESTING WISELY FOR RETIREMENT

Understanding Investment Risk

When retirement planning, it's crucial to understand that investing isn't just about picking stocks or throwing money into a retirement account and hoping for the best. It's about understanding the seas you're navigating, the risks involved, and how to steer your ship wisely through them.

Investment risk is the potential for loss or the variability in the returns of your investments. It's an inherent part of investing; with it, there is potential for higher returns that can help you achieve your retirement goals. However, not all risks are created equal and don't need to be feared; they need to be understood and managed.

There are several types of investment risks that you should be aware of:

- **Market Risk:** This is the risk that the value of your investments will decrease due to economic developments or other events that affect the entire market. The 2008 financial crisis is a prime example of market risk.
- **Interest Rate Risk:** This risk is associated with fixed-income securities, like bonds. When interest rates rise, the value of existing bonds typically falls since new bonds are likely to be issued at a higher rate.
- **Credit Risk:** This is the risk that the bond issuer could default on their payments. Bonds with lower credit ratings are considered riskier but may offer higher returns to compensate.
- **Inflation Risk:** The danger here is that the purchasing power of your money declines. If your investments keep up with inflation, you could gain ground financially even if you realize it.
- **Liquidity Risk:** This is the risk that you may not be able to sell your investment at a fair price and get your money out when you want to. Some investments, like real estate, have higher liquidity risk than others.
- **Horizon Risk:** The risk that your investment horizon may be shortened because of an unforeseen event, such as job loss or illness, forcing you to sell investments that you were expecting to hold for the long term.

- **Longevity Risk:** The flip side of horizon risk is the chance you will outlive your savings. This is particularly relevant for retirees who need to ensure their retirement savings last.

Understanding these risks is the first step in managing them. It's not about avoiding risk altogether—that's nearly impossible and can lead to missed opportunities. Instead, it's about finding the right balance between risk and return that aligns with your retirement goals, time horizon, and comfort level.

Remember, all investments carry some risk, and it's essential to recognize that risk is a natural part of the investing process. By acknowledging and understanding the risks associated with investing, you can make more informed decisions that align with your long-term retirement strategy. This knowledge will serve as a foundation as you learn about diversification and asset allocation, which are key strategies in managing investment risk and are discussed in the following section.

Diversification and Asset Allocation

Now that we've grasped the concept of investment risk in the previous section, it's time to build on that foundation by exploring two critical strategies for managing risk and aiming for a successful retirement: **diversification** and **asset allocation**.

Diversification is often summed up by the old saying, "Don't put all your eggs in one basket." In the context of investing for retirement, this means spreading your investments across various asset classes, such as stocks, bonds, and cash, and within asset classes, like different sectors and geographies. By doing so, you're not overly reliant on the performance of a single investment. If one investment or sector underperforms, another might do well, potentially offsetting losses and reducing the volatility of your portfolio.

Think of diversification as a balancing act. If you were to walk across a tightrope with a pole, the length and weight of the pole help you maintain balance. Each investment in your portfolio acts like a weight on that pole, contributing to a steadier journey across the financial tightrope to retirement.

On the other hand, asset allocation is the process of deciding how to distribute your investments among different asset classes. Unlike diversification, which is about spreading investments within an asset class, asset allocation is about the strategic mix of different asset classes. Your asset allocation should reflect your risk tolerance, investment horizon, and financial goals.

For instance, if you're young and decades away from retirement, you might opt for a more aggressive allocation, with a higher percentage in stocks, which have historically offered higher returns but come with more volatility. As you approach retirement, you might shift towards a more conservative allocation, with more bonds and cash, which tend to offer lower returns but are generally less volatile.

It's important to note that there's no one-size-fits-all asset allocation. It's a personal decision that should be revisited periodically, especially as you reach different stages in your life or if your goals change. Moreover, asset allocation is not a set-it-and-forget-it strategy. It requires regular rebalancing to ensure your portfolio stays aligned with your desired risk level. As market movements may cause your initial allocation to drift, rebalancing helps you sell high and buy low, realigning your portfolio back to your target allocation.

Incorporating diversification and asset allocation into your retirement planning can help you navigate the market's uncertainties while keeping you on track to your long-term objectives. By understanding and applying these concepts, you can create a robust framework for your investment decisions, which we will continue to build upon as we explore the various investment vehicles available.

Remember, the key to investing wisely for retirement is not just about selecting suitable investments but also about how you structure and manage your portfolio over time.

Exploring Investment Vehicles

As we delve into the world of investing for retirement, it's essential to understand the various investment vehicles available to you. These are the tools you will use to build your retirement portfolio, and each comes with its own set of features, risks, and potential rewards. Let's explore some of the most common investment vehicles to help you grow your nest egg.

Firstly, there are stocks, which represent ownership in a company. When you buy a stock, you buy a small piece of that company. Stocks have the potential for high returns, but they also come with a higher risk level than other investment vehicles. The value of stocks can fluctuate significantly based on the company's performance and market conditions. For retirement planning, it's often wise to consider stocks as a long-term investment, allowing you to ride out the ups and downs of the market.

Mutual funds are another popular choice for retirement savings. These funds pool money from many investors to purchase a diversified portfolio of stocks, bonds, or other securities. This diversification can help reduce risk, as your investment isn't tied to the performance of a single security. Mutual funds are managed by professional fund managers, which can be a boon for investors who prefer a hands-off approach. However, it's essential to be aware of the fees associated with mutual funds, as they can eat into your returns over time.

Exchange-traded funds (ETFs) are similar to mutual funds because they offer a diversified portfolio. Still, they trade on an exchange like a stock. This means they can be bought and sold throughout the trading day at market price. ETFs often have lower expense ratios than mutual funds, making them a cost-effective option for many investors. They also offer transparency, as the holdings of an ETF are typically disclosed daily.

Certificates of Deposit (CDs) might appeal to those seeking a more conservative investment vehicle. CDs are time deposits banks offer with a fixed interest rate and maturity date. They are insured by the Federal Deposit Insurance Corporation (FDIC) up to certain limits, making them a low-risk investment. However, the trade-off for this security is typically a lower return compared to stocks or mutual funds.

Another conservative option is Treasury securities, debt instruments issued by the U.S. government. These include Treasury bonds, notes, and bills, and they are considered one of the safest investments since the full faith and credit of the U.S. government backs them. The returns on these securities are usually lower than more aggressive investments, but they can provide a stable income stream and are free from state and local income taxes.

Lastly, there are Individual Retirement Accounts (IRAs) and employer-sponsored plans like 401(k)s, which are not investment vehicles per se but accounts that hold investments. These accounts offer tax advantages that can help your savings grow more efficiently. Within these accounts, you can hold various investment vehicles mentioned above, and choosing the right mix is critical to a successful retirement strategy.

Each investment vehicle has its place in a retirement portfolio, and the right choice for you will depend on your financial goals, risk tolerance, and investment timeline. As you consider your options, remember that a well-rounded portfolio often includes a mix of these vehicles, allowing you to balance potential returns with appropriate levels of risk.

In the next part of our journey, we'll focus on a specific type of investment vehicle that plays a crucial role in many retirement portfolios: bonds. Understanding how bonds work and their benefits will help refine your retirement investment strategy further.

The Role of Bonds in Your Portfolio

When planning to retire, understanding the role of various investment vehicles is crucial. After exploring the broad spectrum of options available, it's time to focus on a critical component that often forms the bedrock of a retirement portfolio: bonds.

Bonds are loans you, as an investor, provide to governments or corporations. In return for your investment, the issuer promises to pay you back the principal amount on a specified maturity date, along with periodic interest payments, known as coupons. These fixed-income securities can serve multiple purposes in your retirement portfolio.

Firstly, bonds are traditionally seen as a safer investment compared to stocks. While they typically offer lower returns, they also come with reduced volatility. This stability is particularly appealing as you approach retirement age and your risk tolerance diminishes. The predictable income stream from bonds can provide peace of mind, knowing that a portion of your retirement funds is insulated from the extreme ups and downs of the stock market.

Another advantage of including bonds in your portfolio is diversification. By spreading your investments across different asset classes, you can mitigate risk. When the stock market is down, bonds often perform differently. This non-correlated behavior can help cushion your portfolio against significant losses.

Bonds also offer tax advantages, mainly if you invest in municipal bonds. These bonds are typically exempt from federal taxes and, in some cases, state and local taxes. This tax efficiency can be beneficial for retirees who are looking to maximize their after-tax income.

However, it's important to note that bonds are not entirely risk-free. They are subject to interest rate, credit, and inflation risks. When interest rates rise, the value of existing bonds typically falls, since new bonds are likely to be issued at higher rates. Credit risk involves the possibility that the bond issuer may default on their payments. Lastly, inflation risk is the threat that the return on bonds may not keep up with the rising cost of living.

To manage these risks, consider the duration and quality of the bonds you select. Shorter-duration bonds are less sensitive to interest rate changes, and high-quality bonds, such as those with higher credit ratings, are less likely to default.

Incorporating bonds into your retirement portfolio requires a strategic approach. You must assess your financial situation, risk tolerance, and retirement goals. A well-constructed bond portfolio can help you balance risk and return, ensuring a more stable and predictable path toward a comfortable retirement.

As you continue your retirement planning journey, remember that the investment landscape is not static. Your portfolio needs periodic adjustments to align with your evolving needs and market conditions. This brings us to the importance of rebalancing your investments, a topic we will explore in the following discussion.

When to Rebalance Your Investments

In retirement planning, understanding the role of bonds is just one piece of the puzzle. Another critical aspect is knowing when and how to rebalance your investments to maintain a healthy, risk-adjusted portfolio. Rebalancing is the process of realigning the weightings of a portfolio of assets to stay in line with your intended asset allocation.

Imagine your retirement portfolio as a garden. When you first plant it, you carefully decide how much of each type of plant (or investment) you want. Over time, some plants may grow faster than others. If left unchecked, these might overshadow the smaller plants, disrupting the balance of your garden. Similarly, one type of investment outperforms others in a portfolio. In that case, it can become a more significant proportion of your portfolio than you originally intended, potentially exposing you to more risk than you're comfortable with.

So, when should you roll up your sleeves and rebalance your investment garden? There are two main strategies to consider:

1. **Time-based rebalancing:** This approach involves checking your portfolio at regular intervals, such as annually or semi-annually, and adjusting as necessary to return to your original asset allocation. This method is straightforward and can be quickly scheduled. However, it doesn't account for significant market movements that may occur between your set rebalancing dates.
2. **Threshold-based rebalancing:** With this strategy, you decide on a specific percentage point that your assets can deviate from their target allocation before rebalancing. For example, if your target allocation is 60% stocks and 40% bonds, you might rebalance if either asset class shifts by more than 5%. This method responds more to market conditions but requires more frequent portfolio monitoring.

Regardless of your chosen strategy, it's important to remember that rebalancing can incur transaction fees and tax implications. To minimize these costs, consider using dividends or new contributions to adjust your portfolio's balance rather than selling off assets.

Rebalancing is not just about reducing risk; it's also about taking advantage of opportunities to buy low and sell high. By selling assets that have appreciated and buying those that have not, you often buy the underperforming assets at a lower price and sell the overperforming ones at a higher price.

In conclusion, regular rebalancing is a disciplined way to

maintain your desired risk level and ensure that your retirement portfolio stays aligned with your long-term financial goals. It's a simple yet powerful tool in your retirement planning toolkit that can help you stay on course through the ups and downs of the market. Remember, the key to successful rebalancing is to have a clear, predefined strategy and to stick to it, allowing you to make decisions based on logic, rather than emotion.

Chapter Summary

- Investing for retirement involves understanding and managing investment risks, not avoiding them.
- Investment risks include market, interest rate, credit, inflation, liquidity, horizon, and longevity risks.
- Diversification and asset allocation are critical strategies for managing investment and balancing risk and return.
- Diversification spreads investments across various asset classes and sectors to reduce reliance on any single investment.
- Asset allocation is a portfolio's strategic mix of asset classes, reflecting risk tolerance and investment goals.
- Retirement investment vehicles include stocks, mutual funds, ETFs, CDs, Treasury securities, IRAs, and 401(k)s.
- Bonds provide a stable income stream and can be safer than stocks, offering diversification and tax advantages.
- Rebalancing investments is crucial to maintain the desired asset allocation, manage risk, and align with financial goals.

3

SOCIAL SECURITY AND OTHER
RETIREMENT INCOME

How Social Security Works

Understanding the mechanics of Social Security is a cornerstone of retirement planning. As you approach this significant phase of life, it's crucial to grasp how this program operates, as it will likely form a substantial part of your retirement income.

Social Security is a federal program designed to provide

financial support to retirees, as well as to individuals with disabilities and survivors of deceased workers. The funding for Social Security comes from payroll taxes paid by workers and their employers, known as the Federal Insurance Contributions Act (FICA) tax. Suppose you've ever glanced at your paycheck and noticed a deduction for FICA. In that case, that's your contribution to the Social Security pool.

Eligibility for retirement benefits under Social Security is based on accumulating credits during your working years. As of the latest guidelines, you earn one credit for a specific amount of earnings, with the amount required for a credit subject to change each year. You can earn up to four credits per year and generally need 40 credits, equivalent to 10 years of work, to qualify for retirement benefits.

Your Social Security benefit amount is calculated based on your 35 highest-earning years. If you have not worked for 35 years, zeros are added to the equation, which can significantly lower your average. The Social Security Administration (SSA) uses a formula to determine your primary insurance amount (PIA), the basis for your benefits.

One of the most critical decisions you'll make regarding Social Security is when to start taking benefits. You can begin receiving benefits as early as age 62, but doing so will reduce your monthly benefit amount because you're taking it over a more extended period. Full retirement age (FRA) varies depending on your birth year, and it's the age at which you're entitled to 100% of your calculated benefit. For those born in 1960 or later, the FRA is 67. Suppose you need to take benefits past your FRA. In that case, your benefit will increase by a certain percentage until you reach age 70, after which there's no additional increase for delay.

It's also important to note that your Social Security benefits may be subject to federal income taxes, depending on your combined income, which includes your adjusted gross income, nontaxable interest, and half of your Social Security benefits.

Understanding these tax implications is essential for planning your retirement income strategy.

In addition to retirement benefits, Social Security also offers spousal benefits, which allow a lower-earning spouse to receive up to 50% of the higher earner's benefit at FRA, and survivor benefits, which provide support to the family members of a deceased worker. Disability benefits are also available, offering income to those who cannot work due to a qualifying disability.

As you can see, Social Security is a multifaceted program with various rules and options that can significantly impact your retirement planning. By comprehending how Social Security works, you can make informed decisions that align with your financial goals and retirement vision. With this foundational knowledge, you'll be better prepared to delve into strategies to maximize your Social Security benefits, ensuring you optimize this vital resource for retirement.

Maximizing Your Social Security Benefits

Having gained an understanding of how Social Security works, it's time to delve into strategies to maximize these benefits, which can significantly impact your financial comfort in retirement. Social Security benefits are not one-size-fits-all; they vary depending on when you start receiving them and your work history. Here, we'll explore practical steps to ensure you get the most out of Social Security.

Firstly, consider the timing of your claim. You can start receiving Social Security benefits as early as age 62, but doing so will reduce your monthly payments because you're taking them longer. For each year you delay your claim past your full retirement age (which varies depending on your birth year), your benefits will increase until you reach age 70. This increase is known as delayed retirement credits. It can be a powerful tool for maximizing your income in later years.

Next, reviewing your earnings record with the Social Security Administration (SSA) is essential. Your benefits are calculated based on your 35 highest-earning years. If there are any errors or unreported income, correcting these can increase your monthly benefit. You can check your earnings record by creating an account on the SSA website.

There are additional considerations for those who are married, divorced, or widowed. Spouses can claim benefits based on their work record or up to 50% of their higher-earning spouse's benefit, whichever is greater. Divorced individuals may also be eligible for benefits based on an ex-spouse's record if the marriage lasted at least ten years. Widows and widowers can receive survivor benefits, a significant portion of the deceased spouse's benefit. Understanding these options can help you make informed decisions that optimize your retirement income.

Another tactic is to coordinate benefits with your spouse if you're married. Couples can maximize their total benefits by staggering their claiming ages. For example, the lower-earning spouse might start benefits earlier, while the higher-earning spouse delays claiming to accrue delayed retirement credits. This strategy increases the higher earner's benefit and sets up the surviving spouse for higher survivor benefits in the future.

Lastly, it's essential to consider how working in retirement affects your Social Security benefits. Suppose you claim benefits before reaching full retirement age and continue to work. In that case, your benefits may be temporarily reduced if your earnings exceed certain thresholds. However, once you reach full retirement age, these earnings limits no longer apply, and your benefit may be recalculated to account for the months when benefits were withheld.

In conclusion, maximizing your Social Security benefits involves careful planning and a clear understanding of the rules. By considering the timing of your claim, ensuring your earnings record is accurate, understanding spousal benefits, coordinating with your spouse, and knowing how continued work affects your benefits, you can make informed decisions that bolster your retirement income. Remember, each person's situation is unique, so consulting with a financial advisor to tailor a strategy that fits your specific needs may be beneficial.

As we move forward, we'll explore other sources of retirement income, such as pensions and annuities, to provide a comprehensive picture of how to secure your financial future during your golden years.

Pensions and Annuities Explained

Beyond the foundational layer provided by Social Security, pensions and annuities stand as two critical pillars of retirement income that can offer stability and predictability. Understanding how these financial vehicles work is essential for anyone plotting toward a secure retirement.

Pensions, often associated with government and union jobs, are defined benefit plans. This means your retirement payout is predetermined based on your salary, years of service, and the specific formula your employer uses. If you're fortunate enough to have a pension, it's like having a promise from your employer to pay you a certain amount each month once you retire. This can be a powerful asset, as it provides a steady stream of income you can count on, much like Social Security, but typically from a private source.

However, pensions are becoming less common as employers shift toward defined contribution plans, like 401(k)s, which place the onus of saving and investing on the employees. If you have a pension, it's essential to understand the terms, such as whether your spouse has an option for survivor benefits and whether the pension is inflation-protected.

On the other hand, annuities are insurance products you can purchase to provide another layer of income in retirement. You can buy an annuity with a lump sum or through a series of payments. In return, the insurance company promises to make periodic payments to you immediately or at some point in the future. Annuities can be complex, with various types offering different features, such as fixed, variable, and indexed annuities.

Fixed annuities provide regular, guaranteed payments, making them predictably similar to pensions. Variable annuities, meanwhile, allow your payments to fluctuate based on the performance of the investment options you choose, which means they can offer growth potential but also come with more risk. Indexed annuities are a hybrid, offering a combination of guaranteed minimum payments with additional earnings that may be tied to a market index.

When considering an annuity, it's crucial to understand the fees involved, the insurance company's financial strength, and the contract's specific terms, such as surrender charges and the death benefit. Annuities can be a valuable tool for guaranteeing a portion of your retirement income. Still, they're only suitable for some and can be pretty complicated.

Both pensions and annuities offer unique benefits and considerations. As you plan for retirement, weigh these options carefully and consider how they might fit into your overall strategy for income in your golden years. Remember, the goal is to build a diversified portfolio of income sources, so you rely on only a few. With careful planning, pensions and annuities can both play a role in helping you achieve a comfortable and secure retirement.

Other Sources of Retirement Income

As we navigate the retirement planning journey, understanding the various streams of income that can support you in your golden years is crucial. Beyond pensions and annuities, which provide structured payouts, several other sources of retirement income can bolster your financial Security.

Firstly, personal savings and investments play a pivotal role. These may include savings accounts, certificates of deposit (CDs), stocks, bonds, mutual funds, and exchange-traded funds (ETFs). The key to maximizing these assets is to start saving early, invest wisely, and manage your portfolio according to your risk tolerance and time horizon. Diversification across different asset classes can help mitigate risk and provide a more stable financial foundation.

Real estate investments can also contribute to your retirement income. Whether it's rental income from a property you own or profits from selling real estate that has appreciated, this can be a significant source of funds. However, it's essential to consider the responsibilities and risks associated with being a landlord and the liquidity of real estate assets.

For those with entrepreneurial spirits, a small business or a side hustle can continue to provide income into retirement. Whether consulting in your field of expertise or turning a hobby into a profitable venture, this can be financially and personally rewarding. However, planning for the eventual transition out of the business is essential, whether selling it, passing it on to family members, or winding it down.

Another often overlooked source of income is a life insurance policy. Some policies have a cash value component that can be borrowed against or withdrawn during retirement. While this should be approached cautiously, as it can affect the death benefit and may have tax implications, it can be a helpful resource in certain situations.

Lastly, you must consider any inheritances or windfalls you may receive. While these should not be relied upon as a primary source of retirement income, they can provide a comfortable cushion or enable you to leave a legacy for your heirs.

Each income source has its considerations, such as tax implications, growth potential, and risks. It's essential to consult with a financial advisor to understand how these pieces fit into your overall retirement plan and how they can be optimized to ensure a stable and comfortable retirement.

By thoughtfully combining these various sources of income with the foundational support of Social Security, pensions, and annuities, you can create a robust and flexible financial strategy that adapts to your changing needs throughout retirement.

Integrating Social Security with Other Retirement Funds

As you embark on retirement planning, understanding how to blend Social Security benefits with other retirement funds is a pivotal step in ensuring a stable financial future. Social Security, while a cornerstone of many retirement plans, is not designed to be the sole source of income once you retire. Instead, it's intended to work with other savings and investment strategies to provide a comprehensive income stream.

To integrate Social Security effectively with other retirement funds, it's crucial to consider when you choose to start receiving benefits. The age at which you begin to collect Social Security can significantly impact your overall retirement strategy. You can start receiving benefits as early as age 62, but doing so may reduce your monthly benefit amount. On the other hand, delaying benefits until your full retirement age—or even up to age 70—can increase your monthly payments.

When planning the integration, evaluating your entire retirement portfolio is essential. This includes personal savings, such as 401(k) plans, IRAs, pensions, and any other investments or income sources you may have. Each of these will play a role in determining the optimal time to tap into Social Security.

One strategy to consider is using your retirement savings to bridge the gap if you delay Social Security benefits. Doing so allows your Social Security benefits to grow while drawing from your other funds. However, this approach requires careful planning to ensure that your savings are sufficient to support you during this period and that your resources are manageable.

Another essential aspect to consider is tax implications. Social Security benefits may be taxable depending on your combined income, which includes adjusted gross income, nontaxable interest, and half of your Social Security benefits. Understanding how your other retirement income sources will affect your tax situation is essential, as it may influence the decision on when to begin taking Social Security benefits.

Additionally, if you plan to work during retirement, you should know how your earnings may affect your Social Security benefits. Suppose you're younger than full retirement age and earn more than the yearly earnings limit. In that case, your Social Security benefits may be reduced. However, once you reach full retirement age, you can earn any amount without affecting your Social Security benefits.

In summary, integrating Social Security with other retirement funds requires a personalized approach that considers your financial needs, life expectancy, and the impact on your overall tax situation. It's a balancing act between the present and the future, ensuring you have enough income to enjoy your retirement years while preserving your financial resources for the long term. Working with a financial advisor can help you navigate these decisions and develop a tailored plan that aligns with your retirement goals.

Chapter Summary

- Social Security is a federal program funded by payroll taxes that provides financial support to retirees, disabled individuals, and survivors of deceased workers.

- Eligibility for retirement benefits is based on credits earned during working years, with 40 credits (10 years of work) typically needed to qualify.
- Benefits are calculated from the 35 highest-earning years, and starting benefits early (age 62) reduces the monthly amount while delaying past full retirement age (FRA) increases it.
- Social Security benefits may be taxed depending on combined income, and the program also offers spousal, survivor, and disability benefits.
- Maximizing benefits involves considering the timing of claims, ensuring accurate earnings records, understanding spousal benefits, and coordinating with a spouse's benefits.
- Pensions are defined benefit plans providing a predetermined monthly payout, while annuities are insurance products offering periodic payments.
- Other retirement income sources include personal savings, investments, real estate, small businesses, life insurance policies, and inheritances.
- Integrating Social Security with other retirement funds involves careful planning around the timing of benefits, tax implications, and the use of personal savings to delay claiming Social Security potentially.

4

TAX PLANNING FOR RETIREMENT

Understanding Retirement Tax Implications

In retirement planning, it's essential to grasp the tax implications that come with it. Unfortunately, taxes don't retire when you do, and understanding how they can affect your retirement income is crucial in ensuring a comfortable retirement.

Firstly, it's essential to recognize that not all retirement income is taxed equally. The government offers certain tax breaks on retirement savings to encourage individuals to save for their golden years. However, once you start withdrawing from your retirement funds, those withdrawals are often considered taxable income.

The type of retirement account you have plays a significant role in how your savings are taxed. Traditional retirement accounts like 401(k)s and traditional IRAs offer tax benefits upfront. Contributions to these accounts are made with pre-tax dollars, which means they reduce your taxable income for the year you contribute. However, when you retire and begin to take distributions, those withdrawals are taxed as ordinary income.

On the other hand, Roth IRAs and 401(k)s are funded with after-tax dollars. This means you don't get a tax deduction for your contributions. The trade-off is that these accounts offer tax-free growth and tax-free withdrawals in retirement, provided certain conditions are met.

It's also worth noting that the timing of your withdrawals can have tax implications. For most retirement accounts, you must start taking minimum distributions, or Required Minimum Distributions (RMDs), by age 72. Not taking these distributions on time can result in hefty penalties.

Another aspect to consider is the tax bracket you expect to be in during retirement. If you anticipate a lower tax bracket, the upfront tax break from a traditional retirement account might be more beneficial. Conversely, if you expect to be in a higher tax bracket, the tax-free withdrawals from a Roth account could be more advantageous.

Social Security benefits also come with their own set of tax rules. Depending on your total income in retirement, a portion of your Social Security benefits may be taxable. Planning your retirement income strategically can help minimize the taxes on these benefits.

Lastly, it's essential to consider the impact of state taxes on your retirement income. Some states offer generous tax breaks for retirees, including no tax on Social Security benefits or exemptions on other types of retirement income. Others may have more stringent tax policies.

In summary, understanding the tax implications of your retirement savings and income is vital to retirement planning. By being aware of how different types of retirement accounts are taxed, the rules around withdrawals, and the potential taxes on Social Security benefits, you can make informed decisions that will help maximize your retirement income and minimize your tax liability. With careful planning and a solid strategy, you can navigate the tax landscape of retirement and secure a more financially stable future.

Tax-Advantaged Retirement Accounts

It's essential to understand the role of tax-advantaged retirement accounts when thinking about retirement planning. These financial vehicles are designed to encourage retirement savings by offering tax benefits that can significantly impact your long-term savings growth. Let's explore the most common types of these accounts and how they can be integrated into your retirement strategy. Note that many of these accounts have been mentioned earlier.

Firstly, we have the traditional Individual Retirement Account (IRA). Contributions to a traditional IRA may be tax-deductible depending on your income, filing status, and other factors. The money in the account grows tax-deferred, meaning you won't pay taxes on the gains until you withdraw the funds in retirement. This can be a powerful tool because it allows your investments to compound over time without the drag of annual taxes.

Another option is the Roth IRA, which takes a different approach. Contributions to a Roth IRA are made with after-tax dollars, meaning you don't get an immediate tax deduction. However, the trade-off is that the withdrawals you make after age 59½ are tax-free, provided the account has been open for at least five years. This can be particularly advantageous if you expect to be in a higher tax bracket in retirement or prefer the certainty of tax-free income later on.

For those who are employed, 401(k) plans are a staple of retirement savings. Offered by many employers, these plans allow you to contribute pre-tax income directly from your paycheck, which then grows tax-deferred. Some employers even match a portion of your contributions, accelerating your savings. Similar to a traditional IRA, you'll pay taxes on the money when you withdraw it in retirement. There are also Roth 401(k) options that mirror the tax treatment of Roth IRAs, offering tax-free withdrawals in exchange for preceding a tax deduction on contributions.

The Simplified Employee Pension (SEP) IRA and the Savings Incentive Match Plan for Employees (SIMPLE) IRA are tailored options for small business owners and self-employed individuals. SEP IRAs allow for higher contribution limits than traditional IRAs, making them suitable for those with higher incomes looking to save more for retirement. SIMPLE IRAs are designed for small businesses and offer employer and employee contributions, providing a collaborative approach to retirement savings.

It's also worth noting that Health Savings Accounts (HSAs) can be a part of your retirement tax strategy. While HSAs are primarily intended for medical expenses, they offer triple tax advantages: contributions are tax-deductible, the money grows tax-free, and withdrawals for qualified medical expenses are tax-free. After age 65, you can withdraw funds for any purpose without penalty. However, you'll pay income taxes on withdrawals not used for qualified medical expenses.

Each account has its rules regarding contributions, income limits, and withdrawals. When choosing the proper tax-advantaged retirement account, consider your current tax bracket, expected future income, and whether you prefer to pay taxes now or later. The goal is to minimize your tax burden throughout your lifetime, not just in the current year.

By strategically using these tax-advantaged accounts, you can build a retirement savings plan that supports your future financial security and optimizes your tax situation. Remember, the key is to start early and contribute consistently, allowing the power of tax-deferred or tax-free growth to work in your favor over the long term. With careful planning and an understanding of these accounts, you can confidently navigate the path to a comfortable retirement.

Strategies for Tax-Efficient Withdrawals

Understanding how to manage your nest egg tax efficiently is crucial as we navigate the retirement planning journey. After all, it's not just what you save but what you keep after taxes that counts. Let's delve into some strategies that can help you maximize your retirement income by minimizing the tax impact.

Firstly, consider the timing of your withdrawals. Suppose you have a mix of tax-deferred (like traditional IRAs or 401(k)s) and tax-free accounts (such as Roth IRAs). In that case, you have some control over your taxable income each year. A common strategy is to pull funds from your tax-deferred accounts up to the top of a tax bracket, ensuring you're not tipping into a higher bracket with additional withdrawals. Then, you can supplement your income with tax-free withdrawals from a Roth IRA, which do not count towards your taxable income.

Another critical strategy is to manage your required minimum distributions (RMDs). Once you reach age 72, you must start taking RMDs from your tax-deferred accounts. These mandatory withdrawals can push you into a higher tax bracket. However, suppose you start taking distributions in your 60s. In that case, you can spread the taxable income over more years, potentially reducing the yearly tax hit.

Consider the potential benefits of converting a traditional IRA to a Roth IRA. This move can be advantageous if you expect to be in a higher tax bracket in the future or if you want to leave tax-free money to your heirs. The conversion will trigger a tax bill, but the money grows tax-free, and withdrawals are tax-free in retirement.

Asset location is another aspect of tax-efficient withdrawal strategies. It involves being strategic about where you hold different types of investments. For example, it's generally more tax-efficient to hold income-generating investments, like bonds, in tax-deferred accounts, where the interest they generate won't be taxed until you withdraw the money. Conversely, holding investments that generate capital gains, like stocks, in taxable accounts can be beneficial since long-term capital gains are taxed at lower rates than ordinary income.

Lastly, pay attention to the impact of state taxes on your retirement withdrawals. If you live in a state with high-income taxes, it might be worth considering how this affects your withdrawal strategy. In some cases, relocating to a state with lower or no income tax could significantly reduce your overall tax burden.

By weaving together these strategies, you can create a tapestry of tax-efficient withdrawals that support a more secure and enjoyable retirement. Remember, the goal is to manage your taxes throughout retirement, not just in the year you retire or when you turn 72. With careful planning and foresight, you can stretch your retirement dollars further and enjoy the fruits of your labor with fewer tax worries.

The Role of Health Savings Accounts (HSAs)

As you navigate the journey toward retirement, understanding the various tools at your disposal for tax planning is crucial. One such tool that often flies under the radar is one that we mentioned in the section before the last: the Health Savings Account or HSA. An HSA is a way to pay for medical expenses and a strategic component in your retirement tax planning arsenal.

An HSA is a tax-advantaged savings account to help individuals save for future medical costs. To be eligible, you must be enrolled in a high-deductible health plan (HDHP). The beauty of an HSA lies in its triple tax advantage: contributions are tax-deductible, the money grows tax-free, and withdrawals for qualified medical expenses are also tax-free.

For those looking toward retirement, an HSA can serve a dual purpose. Initially, it acts as a buffer for current medical expenses, easing the strain on your regular budget. However, its long-term value should be considered. As you age, healthcare costs can become one of the most significant expenses during retirement. An HSA allows you to build a dedicated nest egg for these costs, separate from your other retirement accounts.

The tax benefits of an HSA are particularly compelling. Contributions made to your HSA can be deducted from your taxable income, reducing your overall tax burden for the year. This deduction is available whether you itemize deductions or not. Moreover, the funds in your HSA grow tax-free, which means any interest, dividends, or capital gains accumulate without being subject to tax, much like the growth in a traditional IRA or 401(k).

When it comes to withdrawals, they are not taxed as long as they are used for qualified medical expenses. This includes many costs, from doctor's visits and prescriptions to dental and vision care. Notably, using the funds within a specific time frame is optional. This means you can contribute to your HSA during your working years and allow the account to grow until you need the funds in retirement.

One of the features of Health Savings Accounts (HSAs) is that after you reach age 65, you can withdraw funds for any purpose without incurring a 20% penalty that applies to non-qualified withdrawals before that age. However, suppose the withdrawal is not used for qualified medical expenses. In that case, it will be taxed as income, similar to withdrawals from a traditional IRA. This flexibility adds another layer to your retirement income strategy, providing an additional pool of funds that can be used for non-medical expenses, though with the caveat of being subject to income tax.

It's also worth noting that unlike a Flexible Spending Account (FSA), which has a "use it or lose it" policy, an HSA is portable and rolls over from year to year. If you change jobs or retire, the account remains with you.

Incorporating an HSA into your retirement planning requires a thoughtful approach. Consider how much to contribute each year, considering the annual limits the IRS sets. Also, consider your anticipated healthcare needs and how they may evolve as you age. Balancing contributions to your HSA with contributions to other retirement accounts is critical, as you want to ensure a well-rounded approach to your future financial security.

As you plan for a stable and secure retirement, remember that an HSA is more than just a way to cover current medical expenses —it's a powerful tool that can help you manage your long-term health costs while providing tax benefits that bolster your retirement savings strategy. With careful planning and strategic use, an HSA can be integral to ensuring a comfortable retirement.

Estate Planning and Tax Considerations

As we pivot from the topic of Health Savings Accounts, which offer their own set of tax advantages for medical expenses, let's delve into the realm of estate planning and its tax considerations. Estate planning is a crucial component of retirement planning that can significantly impact the financial legacy you leave behind. It's not just for the wealthy; everyone can benefit from a well-thought-out estate plan.

Firstly, it's essential to understand that estate planning involves more than just drafting a will. It encompasses a range of strategies to manage your assets in life and control their distribution after your passing. A comprehensive estate plan can minimize the tax burden on your heirs, fulfill your wishes, and provide for any dependents you may leave behind.

One of the key tax considerations in estate planning is the federal estate tax, which is levied on the transfer of the taxable estate of a deceased person. As of the time of writing, there is a significant exemption limit before the estate tax kicks in. Still, it's essential to stay updated on current laws as these can change with new legislation.

In addition to federal estate taxes, some states have their own estate or inheritance taxes, which may come with different exemption thresholds. It's crucial to be aware of your state's rules and plan accordingly. Strategies to mitigate these taxes include gifting assets during your lifetime, which can reduce the size of your estate subject to taxation, and setting up trusts that can offer various tax advantages.

Another aspect to consider is the use of beneficiary designations. Assets like retirement accounts and life insurance policies allow you to name beneficiaries directly. These designations typically override what's stated in a will, so keeping them updated and aligned with your estate planning goals is vital.

Furthermore, the tax basis of inherited assets is another important consideration. Generally, heirs receive a "step-up" as a basis for inherited assets, meaning they're valued as of the date of the deceased's death for tax purposes. This can significantly reduce capital gains taxes if the assets are appreciated over time and sold by the heirs.

Lastly, it's essential to consult with a financial advisor or estate planning attorney who can help you navigate the complexities of estate taxes and assist in crafting a plan that suits your needs. They can provide guidance on the use of trusts, charitable giving strategies, and other tools that can be employed to create a tax-efficient estate plan.

Remember, estate planning is not a one-time task but an ongoing process that should be revisited regularly as tax laws and personal circumstances change. By taking a proactive approach to estate planning and understanding the tax implications, you can ensure that your retirement planning is robust and comprehensive and leaves a lasting, positive impact on your loved ones.

Chapter Summary

- Retirement income is taxed differently, and understanding these implications is critical to a comfortable retirement.
- Traditional retirement accounts like 401(k)s and IRAs offer tax benefits upfront but are taxed upon withdrawal.
- Roth IRAs and 401(k)s are funded with after-tax dollars and offer tax-free growth and withdrawals under certain conditions.
- Withdrawals from retirement accounts are often required by age 72, and timing can affect tax brackets and liabilities.
- Social Security benefits may be taxable depending on total income, and state taxes can also impact retirement income.
- Tax-advantaged retirement accounts, such as traditional and Roth IRAs, 401(k)s, SEP IRAs, SIMPLE IRAs, and HSAs, offer various benefits and should be chosen based on individual circumstances.
- Strategies for tax-efficient withdrawals include managing the timing and types of accounts withdrawn

from, considering Roth conversions, and understanding asset location.

- Estate planning is essential for managing assets and minimizing tax burdens for heirs, involving wills, trusts, gifting, and keeping up with tax law changes.

5

HEALTHCARE IN RETIREMENT

Estimating Healthcare Costs in Retirement

As you approach retirement, healthcare is one of the most significant expenses you'll need to plan for. Unlike your younger years, when an employer's health plan may have covered you, retirement brings a new landscape of medical costs that can impact your savings if not appropriately anticipated. To ensure a comfortable retirement, estimating your healthcare costs is a crucial step in your planning process.

Firstly, it's essential to understand that healthcare costs in retirement can vary widely depending on your health, location, and the level of care you require. However, there are some everyday expenses that most retirees can expect to face. These include Medicare Part B and Part D premiums (more on these later), out-of-pocket expenses for co-pays, deductibles, and services not covered by Medicare, as well as costs for supplemental insurance policies.

To get a realistic estimate of your healthcare costs in retirement, start by looking at the current costs of healthcare services and the rate at which they have been increasing. Historically, healthcare costs have risen faster than general inflation, so it's wise to factor in a higher rate of increase for these expenses.

Next, consider your own health status and family medical history. You may face higher healthcare costs if you have chronic conditions or a family history of certain diseases. It's also essential to consider the potential need for long-term care, which can be one of retirement's most significant healthcare-related expenses. Long-term care insurance can help mitigate these costs, but premiums for such policies should be included in your calculations.

Remember to account for the coverage gaps in Medicare. While Medicare will cover many of your healthcare needs, it doesn't cover everything. For example, dental, vision, and hearing services are typically not covered, and traditional Medicare does not cover long-term care. This is where supplemental insurance, often called Medigap, can help fill in the gaps, but at an additional cost.

When estimating your healthcare costs, use available tools and resources. Many online calculators can help you project your healthcare expenses based on your age, health status, and other factors. Additionally, speaking with a financial planner specializing in retirement healthcare can provide personalized insights and help you create a more accurate and comprehensive healthcare budget.

Finally, as you estimate your healthcare costs, reviewing these estimates regularly is essential. As you get closer to retirement and once you are retired, your health needs may change, and healthcare policies and costs may also evolve. Regularly updating your estimates will help you stay on top of your expenses and adjust your savings and investment strategies accordingly.

By carefully estimating your healthcare costs in retirement, you'll be better prepared to enjoy your golden years without the stress of unexpected medical expenses. With a clear understanding of what to expect, you can focus on maintaining your health and well-being, knowing that you've planned wisely for the financial aspect of your healthcare needs.

Medicare Basics

As you edge closer to retirement, understanding the basics of Medicare becomes increasingly essential. Medicare is the federal health insurance program for people who are 65 or older, certain younger people with disabilities, and people with End-Stage Renal Disease (permanent kidney failure requiring dialysis or a transplant). It's a critical component of your retirement healthcare planning, and getting to grips with its structure will help you estimate your healthcare costs and decide on supplemental insurance options.

Medicare is divided into four parts, each covering different services:

- **Medicare Part A (Hospital Insurance):** This part covers inpatient hospital stays, care in a skilled nursing facility, hospice care, and some home health care. Most people don't pay a premium for Part A because they or their spouse have already paid into the system through payroll taxes during their working years.

- **Medicare Part B (Medical Insurance):** Part B covers doctors' services, outpatient care, medical supplies, and preventive services. Unlike Part A, Part B requires a monthly premium based on your income. The standard premium amount changes yearly, and you may pay more if your income is above a certain threshold.
- **Medicare Part C (Medicare Advantage Plans):** These are health plan options approved by Medicare but run by private companies. They are an alternative to Original Medicare (Parts A and B), often including additional benefits like vision, hearing, dental, and health and wellness programs. Most also include Medicare prescription drug coverage (Part D).
- **Medicare Part D (prescription drug coverage):** Part D adds prescription drug coverage to Original Medicare, some Medicare Cost Plans, some Medicare Private-Fee-for-Service Plans, and Medicare Medical Savings Account Plans. These plans are offered by insurance companies and other private companies approved by Medicare.

Enrollment in Medicare is not automatic for everyone. Suppose you are already receiving Social Security benefits. In that case, you will be enrolled automatically in Parts A and B starting the first day of the month you turn 65. Suppose you are not receiving Social Security benefits. In that case, you'll need to sign up for Medicare during your Initial Enrollment Period, which begins three months before you turn 65 and ends three months after that month.

It's essential to sign up for Medicare as soon as you're eligible because if you enroll late, you may have to pay a late enrollment penalty, which could increase your premiums for Part B and Part D. There are specific special enrollment periods for those who are still working and covered under an employer's group health plan, or for those who experience other life changes.

Understanding the basics of Medicare is just the start. You'll also need to consider the additional costs that aren't covered by Medicare, such as copayments, coinsurance, and deductibles. These out-of-pocket costs can add up, highlighting the importance of considering supplemental health insurance to help cover what Medicare does not. You can better plan for a secure and healthy retirement with a solid grasp of Medicare's structure and costs.

Supplemental Health Insurance Options

Understanding Medicare is crucial as you approach retirement, but it's equally important to recognize that Medicare doesn't cover everything. Many retirees turn to supplemental health insurance options to bridge the gaps in coverage and protect against unforeseen health-related expenses. These options can help manage the costs that Medicare does not fully cover, such as copayments, coinsurance, and deductibles.

Medigap, or Medicare Supplement Insurance, is a popular supplemental option. Medigap policies are sold by private insurance companies and are designed to work alongside your Original Medicare (Parts A and B). These policies help pay some healthcare costs that Original Medicare doesn't cover. Several Medigap plans are available, each labeled with a different letter that offers a different level of coverage. It's essential to compare the plans carefully and choose one that fits your health needs and budget.

Another option to consider is Medicare Advantage Plans or Medicare Part C. Private companies approved by Medicare offer these plans and provide all your Part A and Part B coverage. Medicare Advantage Plans may offer extra coverage, like vision, hearing, dental, and health and wellness programs. Most include Medicare prescription drug coverage (Part D). These plans often have networks, so you'll need to ensure your preferred doctors and hospitals are covered under your chosen plan.

For prescription drug coverage, you might consider a Medicare Prescription Drug Plan, also known as Part D. These plans add drug coverage to Original Medicare, some Medicare Cost Plans, some Medicare Private-Fee-for-Service Plans, and Medicare Medical Savings Account Plans. If you have Original Medicare and want drug coverage, you must join a separate Medicare Prescription Drug Plan. These plans vary in cost and drugs covered.

If you or your spouse worked for the government, you might be eligible for the Federal Employees Health Benefits Program. This program offers various plans and options that can be a valuable supplement to Medicare.

When considering supplemental health insurance, evaluating your current health needs, financial situation, and risk tolerance is crucial. Costs vary widely depending on the plan, coverage, and where you live. Review each plan's details, including the premium, deductible, and out-of-pocket maximums, to understand how they fit into your retirement budget.

Remember, the best time to enroll in these supplemental plans is during your initial enrollment period for Medicare, as you may face limited choices or higher premiums if you decide to enroll later. Planning and understanding all your options will help ensure you have the coverage you need to enjoy a healthy and financially secure retirement.

As you continue to navigate the complexities of healthcare in retirement, it's also essential to consider the potential need for long-term care and how it can impact your financial planning. Long-term care insurance is a topic that warrants careful consideration, as it can play a significant role in your overall retirement strategy.

Long-Term Care Insurance

As we navigate the golden years, one aspect of healthcare that often comes into sharper focus is the potential need for long-term care.

Long-term care encompasses a range of services and supports you may require to meet your care needs over a long period. Unlike traditional health insurance, long-term care insurance is designed to cover long-term services, including personal and custodial care, in various settings, such as your home, a community organization, or other facilities.

For many retirees, the question isn't about whether they'll need long-term care but how they'll pay for it if they do. Medicare, the federal health insurance program for seniors, provides limited coverage for long-term care. Medicaid covers such services and requires you to deplete most of your resources before you qualify. This is where long-term care insurance can play a pivotal role.

Long-term care insurance policies can help manage the financial risk of extended care that can otherwise quickly deplete retirement savings. These policies typically cover the cost of care not covered by health insurance, Medicare, or Medicaid, including assistance with activities of daily living such as bathing, dressing, eating, and using the restroom.

When considering long-term care insurance, it's essential to understand the types of policies available:

- **Traditional Policies:** These are stand-alone long-term care policies that require you to pay a premium over time. If you need long-term care, the policy pays out a daily or monthly benefit. If you never need the care, there is no return on the premiums paid.
- **Hybrid Policies:** These combine long-term care and life insurance. You pay a lump sum or make periodic payments, and if you need long-term care, the policy provides a benefit. If you don't need the care, the policy pays out a death benefit to your beneficiaries.
- **Short-Term Care Policies:** These are similar to traditional long-term care policies but have a shorter benefit period, typically one year or less.

When shopping for long-term care insurance, consider the following factors:

- **Age and Health:** The best time to buy a policy is when you are relatively young and healthy. Premiums rise as you age, and if you wait until health issues emerge, you may not qualify for coverage or face prohibitively high premiums.
- **Benefit Amount:** Determine how much coverage you want. This is usually expressed as a daily or monthly benefit, and it should align with the cost of care in your area.
- **Benefit Period:** Decide how long you want the policy to pay out. This could range from a couple of years to the rest of your life.
- **Inflation Protection:** Since the cost of care will likely increase over time, consider a policy that includes inflation protection to ensure that your benefits keep pace with rising costs.
- **Waiting Period:** The elimination period is when you become eligible for benefits, and the policy starts paying out. A longer waiting period can mean lower premiums, but you'll need to cover your costs.
- **Financial Strength of the Insurer:** Choose a company with a solid financial rating, as this indicates their ability to pay claims in the future.

Remember, long-term care insurance isn't the right choice for everyone. It's a complex product and requires a good deal of foresight and financial planning. Weigh the costs against the potential benefits and consider your risk tolerance and retirement savings. Consulting with a financial advisor or an insurance specialist can provide personalized advice tailored to your circumstances.

By understanding and planning for the potential need for long-term care, you can ensure that you can maintain your independence and quality of life in retirement while protecting your savings and providing peace of mind for yourself and your loved ones.

Managing Out-of-Pocket Healthcare Expenses

As we navigate the waters of retirement, a significant concern often surfaces: the management of out-of-pocket healthcare expenses. While we've discussed the role of long-term care insurance in the previous section, it's equally important to understand the broader spectrum of healthcare costs you may encounter during retirement.

Firstly, it's crucial to grasp what out-of-pocket healthcare expenses encompass. Medicare or other health insurance plans don't cover these costs. They include deductibles, copayments, and coinsurance for covered services, plus all costs for services that aren't covered.

To effectively manage these expenses, consider the following strategies:

- **Understand Medicare Coverage:** Continue familiarizing yourself with what Medicare covers and doesn't. Parts A and B cover hospital and medical costs, respectively, but they don't cover everything. For instance, routine dental and vision care should be covered. Knowing these details can help you plan for additional coverage.
- **Medigap Policies:** These supplemental insurance policies are designed to cover the "gaps" in Medicare, such as deductibles and coinsurance. Compare Medigap plans to find one that aligns with your healthcare needs and budget.

- **Medicare Advantage Plans:** Alternatively, you might consider a Medicare Advantage Plan (Part C) as mentioned earlier, which often includes additional benefits like dental, vision, and prescription drug coverage. These plans can reduce out-of-pocket expenses but include rules, restrictions, and costs.
- **Health Savings Account (HSA):** Again, if you have a high-deductible health plan before retiring, you might have access to an HSA. Contributions to an HSA are tax-deductible and grow tax-free, and withdrawals for qualified medical expenses are tax-free. If you're eligible, maximize your contributions before retirement.
- **Budgeting for Healthcare:** Create a detailed budget that includes healthcare costs. Use your current health status and anticipated needs to estimate expenses. Remember to factor in inflation, as healthcare costs tend to rise faster than the general inflation rate.
- **Preventive Care:** Staying healthy can help reduce healthcare costs. Take advantage of preventive services offered by Medicare, such as annual wellness visits and screenings. Preventive care can help catch health issues early when they are more manageable and less costly.
- **Lifestyle Choices:** Adopting a healthy lifestyle can significantly impact healthcare costs. Regular exercise, a balanced diet, and avoiding tobacco can reduce the risk of chronic diseases that are expensive to treat.
- **Emergency Fund:** Even with the best planning, unexpected healthcare costs can arise. An emergency fund specifically for health-related expenses can provide a financial buffer.
- **Review and Adjust:** Your health needs will change over time, and so will healthcare policies and costs. Regularly review your healthcare coverage and expenses. Be prepared to adjust your strategies as necessary.

By taking these steps, you can exert greater control over your healthcare expenses in retirement. The goal is to balance the coverage you need and what you can afford, ensuring your golden years are as stress-free and healthy as possible. Remember, managing out-of-pocket healthcare expenses is an ongoing process that requires attention and adjustment as your needs and the healthcare landscape evolve.

Chapter Summary

- Healthcare costs in retirement can vary and include Medicare premiums, out-of-pocket expenses, and supplemental insurance costs.
- Costs have historically risen faster than inflation, so a higher rate of increase should be factored into estimates.
- Personal health status and family medical history can influence costs, and the potential need for long-term care should be considered.
- Medicare has coverage gaps, such as dental, vision, and hearing services, which may require additional Medigap insurance.
- Tools and financial planners can help estimate healthcare expenses, which should be reviewed regularly as circumstances change.
- Medicare is divided into parts A, B, C, and D, covering hospital, medical, advantage plans, and prescription drugs.
- Supplemental insurance options like Medigap, Medicare Advantage Plans, and Part D can help cover costs not fully covered by Medicare.
- Long-term care insurance is essential for covering services not included in traditional health insurance or Medicare.

6

RETIREMENT LIFESTYLE PLANNING

Envisioning Your Retirement Lifestyle

As you approach retirement, it's natural to start dreaming about your life during those golden years. Envisioning your retirement lifestyle is crucial in planning for a fulfilling and satisfying retirement. It's about more than just how you will fill your days; it's about who you will spend them with, where you will live, and what activities will bring you joy and purpose.

Begin by considering the aspects of your current lifestyle you enjoy and would like to carry forward into retirement. Do you love the hustle and bustle of city life, or do you yearn for the tranquility of the countryside? Are there hobbies or passions you've been waiting to explore when you have more time? Perhaps you've wanted to write a novel, learn a new language, or become proficient in painting or gardening. Retirement is the perfect time to dive into these interests.

Think also about your social needs. If you thrive on social interaction, you'll want to ensure that your retirement lifestyle includes plenty of opportunities for engagement with friends, family, and community. This could mean joining clubs, volunteering, or even working part-time in a field you love.

Physical activity is another vital consideration. Regular exercise can help you maintain your health and vitality. Whether golf, yoga, swimming, or walking, find activities you enjoy and can see yourself doing regularly.

Travel often features prominently in retirement dreams. Whether it's long trips to far-flung destinations or shorter excursions closer to home, consider how travel fits into your vision for retirement. Remember to be realistic about your budget and physical capabilities when planning your adventures.

Lastly, consider your day-to-day living environment. The home and community where you choose to spend your retirement years can significantly impact your overall happiness. You can downsize to a smaller, more manageable home or opt for a retirement community offering various amenities and activities. Some retirees even live abroad, seeking new cultural experiences and potentially lowering living costs.

Remember that flexibility is critical as you reflect on your retirement lifestyle. Your interests and circumstances may change, and having a plan that can adapt to you will help ensure that your retirement years are as rewarding as possible. With careful thought and planning, you can craft a retirement lifestyle that reflects your desires and needs, setting the stage for a rich, fulfilling next chapter of life.

Relocation in Retirement: Pros and Cons

As you embark on the exciting retirement journey, one of the pivotal decisions you may face is whether to stay put or relocate. This choice can significantly impact your retirement lifestyle, so carefully weigh the pros and cons.

Here are the pros of relocating during retirement:

- **Cost of Living Adjustments:** Moving to an area with a lower cost of living can stretch your retirement savings. This could mean downsizing to a smaller home or relocating to a region with lower taxes and reduced everyday expenses.
- **Climate and Environment:** Many retirees dream of moving to a place with a more agreeable climate. Whether seeking warmer weather, less humidity, or a desire to live by the ocean or mountains, the right environment can significantly enhance your quality of life.
- **Proximity to Family and Friends:** Relocating can bring you closer to loved ones, providing emotional support and opportunities to create new memories. This can be especially important as you age and prioritize relationships.
- **Access to Healthcare:** As health becomes a more pressing concern, living in an area with excellent healthcare facilities and services can be a significant advantage. Some retirees move to be near specialized

medical centers or communities with robust healthcare
options.

- **Lifestyle Opportunities:** Retirement is a time to explore
new hobbies or reignite past passions. Moving to a
community with like-minded individuals or a place that
offers the cultural, recreational, or educational
opportunities you desire can be invigorating.

Here are the cons of relocating during retirement:

- **Emotional Toll:** Leaving behind a familiar
environment, cherished home, and community ties can
be emotionally challenging. The sense of loss and
nostalgia for the familiar can affect your well-being.
- **Moving Costs and Hassles:** Moving can be daunting,
with packing, selling your home, buying a new one, and
the physical and financial costs associated with the
move itself.
- **Adjustment Period:** Settling into a new community
takes time. Building new friendships, finding your way
around, and establishing new routines can be stressful
and may take longer than anticipated.
- **Unexpected Expenses:** The cost of living in a new
location may have hidden expenses that you didn't
account for, such as higher insurance rates, homeowner
association fees, or property taxes.
- **Healthcare Disruption:** If you have established
relationships with healthcare providers or are in the
midst of ongoing treatments, moving away can disrupt
your care. Finding new doctors and transferring medical
records can be a complex process.

Before leaping to relocate in retirement, it's crucial to consider
these factors in the context of your situation. Take the time to

research potential destinations, visit them, and realistically assess the impact on your finances and emotional well-being. Remember, the goal is to find a place that aligns with your envisioned retirement lifestyle, allowing you to thrive in this new chapter of life.

As you contemplate the possibility of relocating, it's equally important to consider how you'll spend your leisure time and manage travel expenses, which we'll explore in the following section. Your retirement should be a period of joy and fulfillment, and careful planning can help ensure that it is.

Budgeting for Leisure and Travel

The allure of leisure and travel often becomes more pronounced as you approach retirement. After years of hard work, the freedom to explore new places and indulge in hobbies can be advantageous. However, careful budgeting is essential to enjoy these pursuits without financial stress. In this section, we'll delve into how to effectively budget for leisure and travel in retirement, ensuring that your golden years are as fulfilling as you've envisioned.

Firstly, estimating your travel and leisure expenses as part of your overall retirement budget is crucial. Start by considering the types of activities you enjoy. Are you an avid golfer, a theater enthusiast, or a connoisseur of fine dining? You may dream of annual trips abroad or purchasing an RV to explore the country. Each activity carries a different cost profile, and recognizing your preferences will help you allocate funds appropriately.

Next, research the costs associated with your interests. If travel is a priority, look into the expenses for destinations on your bucket list. Consider travel off-season to save money, and remember to factor in travel insurance costs, which becomes increasingly important as we age. For ongoing hobbies, calculate the annual expenses for club memberships, equipment, or tickets to events.

Once you have a clear picture of the costs, it's time to integrate them into your retirement budget. A common strategy is creating a separate 'leisure account' where a portion of your retirement income is automatically deposited monthly. This method makes it easier to track leisure spending and prevents dipping into funds reserved for essential expenses.

It's also wise to consider the fluctuating nature of travel and leisure expenses. Some years, you may spend more, such as when you embark on a significant trip, while other years might be more modest. To accommodate this, you might adopt a multi-year budgeting approach, allowing unused funds from one year to roll over into the next.

Take notice of the potential for unexpected opportunities or changes in interests. A flexible budget can accommodate the occasional splurge or pursuing a new hobby. Additionally, staying informed about discounts for seniors, such as reduced admission fees to parks and museums or travel deals, can stretch your leisure budget further.

Remember, the goal of budgeting for leisure and travel in retirement isn't to restrict your enjoyment but to ensure that you can savor these experiences without financial worry. By planning and setting realistic budgetary boundaries, you can look forward to a retirement filled with the activities and adventures that bring you the most joy.

Staying Active and Engaged

As you transition from the working phase of your life into retirement, it's essential to recognize that staying active and engaged is not just a matter of filling time. It's about nurturing your well-being, both physically and mentally. The newfound freedom of retirement offers a blank canvas upon which you can paint a vibrant, fulfilling, and purposeful lifestyle.

First and foremost, consider the activities that have always brought you joy or those you've yearned to explore but never had the time for. Retirement is the perfect opportunity to dive into these interests. Whether gardening, painting, learning a musical instrument, or writing your memoirs, these activities can provide a sense of accomplishment and joy.

Physical activity is another critical component of an active retirement lifestyle. Regular exercise, tailored to your abilities and interests, can help maintain your health, flexibility, and balance. Joining a local gym, taking up yoga or tai chi, or simply going for daily walks can significantly affect how you feel. Moreover, these activities often provide social benefits, allowing you to connect with others with similar interests.

Social engagement is just as critical as physical activity. Staying connected with friends, family, and your community can help ward off feelings of isolation and loneliness that some retirees experience. Volunteer work is a fantastic way to stay engaged. It helps you give back to the community and provides a sense of purpose and connection. Look for opportunities in local schools, hospitals, or non-profit organizations that resonate with your values and skills.

Learning doesn't stop when your career does. Retirement can be a time of intellectual exploration. Consider enrolling in courses at a local community college or university. Many institutions offer programs specifically for seniors or allow them to audit classes at a reduced rate. Alternatively, online platforms provide a wealth of knowledge on virtually any topic imaginable, from history to computer programming.

Lastly, take into account the importance of downtime. While staying active is crucial, so is taking the time to relax and rejuvenate. Reading, meditating, or enjoying a quiet afternoon in your favorite park are all valuable activities. Balance is vital in retirement, as in any stage of life.

By integrating a mix of physical, social, intellectual, and leisure activities into your retirement plan, you'll be well on your way to a retirement that is not just restful but also stimulating and rewarding. Remember, retirement is not an end but a new beginning, a phase of life where you can design your days with a blend of enjoyable and enriching activities.

Part-Time Work and Entrepreneurship in Retirement

As we embrace the concept of retirement, it's essential to recognize that leaving the workforce doesn't necessarily mean stepping away from all forms of work. Part-time work and entrepreneurship can be incredibly fulfilling components of your retirement lifestyle. Let's explore how these options can supplement your income and enrich your post-career years with purpose and passion.

Part-time work during retirement is an excellent way to stay connected to the professional world without the full-time commitment. It offers flexibility, allowing you to balance leisure with earning a paycheck. For many retirees, part-time jobs provide more than just financial benefits; they offer social interaction, mental stimulation, and a sense of social contribution. When considering part-time work, look for roles that align with your interests or past experiences. You could consult within your former industry or enjoy retail work in a field you're passionate about, like gardening or bookselling.

On the other hand, retirement can be the perfect time to unleash your entrepreneurial spirit. Starting a business can be an exciting venture, allowing you to turn a hobby or a lifelong dream into a source of income. Entrepreneurship in retirement comes with the freedom to set your own pace and make decisions that align with your desired lifestyle. Whether it's starting a small craft business, offering freelance services, or even launching a start-up, the key is choosing an endeavor that you're truly passionate about that won't overburden you.

Before diving into part-time work or entrepreneurship, it's essential to consider how this income will affect your retirement savings and tax situation. Consulting with a financial advisor can help you understand the implications and ensure your work supports your long-term financial security.

Moreover, it's crucial to strike a balance that keeps the leisure time you've earned. Retirement is your time to relax and enjoy life at a slower pace. Ensure that any work you take on enhances your life rather than becoming a source of stress.

Part-time work and entrepreneurship can be rewarding ways to complement your retirement. They provide opportunities to stay active, engaged, and financially secure. By carefully selecting work that aligns with your interests and lifestyle goals, you can craft a productive and pleasurable retirement. Remember, retirement is not the end of your working life; it's a new chapter where you can redefine what work means.

Chapter Summary

- Envisioning your retirement lifestyle is essential for a fulfilling retirement, considering factors like location, social needs, and hobbies.
- Physical activity and travel are essential aspects of retirement planning, with realistic considerations for budget and health.
- Relocating in retirement has pros, such as lower living costs and better climate, and cons, like emotional challenges and moving expenses.
- Budgeting for leisure and travel is crucial to enjoying these activities without financial stress, including estimating costs and creating a separate leisure account.
- Staying active and engaged through hobbies, exercise, socializing, and learning is vital for physical and mental well-being in retirement.
- Downtime is also essential for relaxation, rejuvenation, and a balanced retirement lifestyle.

- Part-time work and entrepreneurship can provide financial benefits, purpose, and passion in retirement, with flexibility and alignment with personal interests.
- It's essential to consider the impact of additional income on retirement savings and taxes and to ensure work doesn't compromise leisure time.

7

PROTECTING YOUR RETIREMENT SAVINGS

Insurance Needs for Retirees

As you approach retirement, it's crucial to understand that your insurance needs may change significantly. While working, you might have relied on employer-provided health insurance, life insurance, and perhaps even disability coverage. However, as you transition into retirement, these safety nets often disappear, necessitating a thorough review of your insurance requirements to protect your hard-earned retirement savings.

Firstly, health insurance becomes a pivotal concern for retirees. Suppose you retire before you are eligible for Medicare at age 65. In that case, you'll need to find an alternative form of health insurance to bridge the gap. Even after you qualify for Medicare, you may want to consider purchasing supplemental insurance, often referred to as Medigap, to cover expenses that Medicare does not, such as copayments, deductibles, and certain types of care.

Long-term care insurance is another important consideration. The cost of long-term care can be staggering and is not typically covered by Medicare. Long-term care insurance can help protect your retirement savings from the potential financial burden of this type of care. However, these policies can be expensive, so weighing the costs and benefits carefully and considering factors such as your health history and family longevity is essential.

Life insurance needs may also change as you enter retirement. If your children are independent and your mortgage is paid off, you might not need as much life insurance as you did when you were younger. However, if you have dependents or significant debts, maintaining life insurance could be wise to protect your loved ones.

Additionally, an often-overlooked type of insurance is liability insurance. As you age, the risk of being sued for accidents on your property or as a result of your actions can threaten your retirement nest egg. An umbrella liability policy can offer extra protection above and beyond your standard homeowners or auto insurance policies.

Finally, it's essential to regularly review and adjust your insurance coverage throughout your retirement to ensure it continues to meet your changing needs. Your health situation can change as you age, and your insurance should adapt accordingly. Working with a financial advisor or insurance professional can help you navigate these complex decisions and find the best coverage.

By carefully considering your insurance needs and ensuring you're adequately protected, you can help safeguard your retirement savings against unforeseen expenses, allowing you to enjoy your golden years with greater peace of mind.

Dealing with Debt Before Retirement

One of the most crucial steps you can take to protect your nest egg is to tackle any outstanding debt. Entering retirement debt-free is not just a matter of financial health—it's also about peace of mind. Let's explore strategies to manage and eliminate debt before you bid farewell to your working years.

Firstly, it's essential to understand the types of debt you have. High-interest debt, such as credit card balances, should be your top priority. These debts can quickly spiral out of control and eat into the savings you've worked so hard to accumulate. Consider transferring balances to a lower-interest card or a consolidation loan, but only if it will help you pay off the debt more quickly and with less interest.

Next, look at any loans or mortgages you may have. While these often come with lower interest rates, they can still be burdensome in retirement. Accelerate your payments now while you have a steady income. Even small additional payments can significantly reduce the interest you'll pay over the life of the loan. You can shorten the time to pay it off.

Another critical step is to create a budget that prioritizes debt repayment. This may mean cutting back on discretionary spending or boosting your income while working. Every extra dollar you can put toward your debt is an investment in your future financial security.

It's also wise to avoid taking on new debt. As retirement nears, you may be tempted to finance that dream vacation or the new car you've been eyeing. However, remember that borrowing money now will only reduce the funds available in retirement if you must make a large purchase. Plan and save for it rather than rely on credit.

If you're struggling to manage your debt, don't hesitate to seek help. A financial advisor can provide personalized advice and help you develop a plan to get back on track. There are also non-profit credit counseling services that can assist with budgeting and debt management plans.

Finally, as you work toward becoming debt-free, it's essential to maintain a safety net. While paying off debt is a priority, you should also ensure an emergency fund is in place. Unforeseen expenses can sometimes arise, and having a reserve can prevent you from falling back into debt.

By addressing your debt before retirement, you're protecting your savings and setting the stage for a more relaxed and enjoyable retirement. With fewer financial obligations, you can focus on the activities and experiences that matter most. Remember, the freedom from debt is one of the most valuable assets you can have in retirement.

Avoiding Scams and Financial Fraud

Safeguarding your nest egg becomes paramount as you approach retirement. After all, you've worked hard to accumulate these savings, representing your financial security during your golden years. Protecting your retirement savings is critical to being vigilant against scams and financial fraud. Unfortunately, unscrupulous individuals often target retirees because they may have substantial savings and can be perceived as less savvy with new technology or financial schemes.

To help you navigate these treacherous waters, let's explore some practical steps you can take to avoid becoming a victim of financial fraud.

Firstly, educate yourself about the common types of scams that target retirees. These can range from investment fraud, such as

Ponzi schemes and fake opportunities promising high returns with little or no risk, to personal scams like phishing attempts or the grandparent scam, where someone pretends to be a relative needing immediate financial help.

Be skeptical of unsolicited offers. If you receive an offer out of the blue, whether through email, a phone call, or even a knock on the door, treat it with caution. Scammers often use high-pressure tactics to create a sense of urgency, so take your time researching and thinking things over before making any financial decisions.

Protect your personal information zealously. Only give out sensitive information such as your Social Security number, bank account details, or credit card numbers if you initiated the contact and know the recipient's legitimacy. Shred documents containing personal information before disposing of them.

Verify credentials and seek independent advice. Before you invest with a new financial advisor or buy an insurance product, check their credentials with regulatory bodies such as the Securities and Exchange Commission (SEC) or the Financial Industry Regulatory Authority (FINRA). Additionally, it's wise to get a second opinion from a trusted financial advisor or a family member when considering significant financial moves.

Monitor your accounts regularly. Keep an eye on your bank and retirement accounts, looking for unauthorized transactions. Setting up alerts for large transactions can also help you stay informed of any significant changes in your account.

Finally, if something sounds too good to be true, it probably is. Be wary of any investment or opportunity that guarantees returns with no risk. The reality is that all investments carry some risk, and those promising otherwise are often red flags for fraud.

By staying informed and cautious, you can significantly reduce the risk of falling prey to scams and ensure that your retirement savings remain secure when needed. Protecting your financial well-being is about growing your savings and preventing losses through vigilance and intelligent decision-making.

The Importance of an Emergency Fund

As you embark on the retirement planning journey, it's crucial to understand that safeguarding your future isn't just about growing your nest egg but also about protecting it from potential setbacks. Establishing an emergency fund is one of the most effective ways to shield your retirement savings. This financial buffer can help you manage unexpected expenses without dipping into the retirement pot you've worked so hard to cultivate.

An emergency fund is a cash reserve readily accessible and earmarked for unforeseen events such as medical emergencies, home repairs, or sudden job loss. The importance of this fund cannot be overstated, as it serves as your first line of defense against the unpredictable nature of life. With it, you may be able to withdraw from your retirement accounts earlier than planned, which can have several adverse effects.

Firstly, early withdrawals can significantly diminish the compound growth of your savings. Remember, the money you pull out today could have grown substantially over time, potentially leaving you with a much smaller sum when you retire. Secondly, taking money out of certain retirement accounts before reaching the age of 59½ often triggers penalties and taxes, further eroding your savings.

So, how much should you aim to save in your emergency fund? A good rule of thumb is to have enough to cover three to six months' living expenses. This amount can provide a comfortable cushion, giving you the peace of mind to handle life's curveballs without jeopardizing your retirement goals.

Building an emergency fund may seem daunting, especially starting from scratch. However, you can gradually build up this critical resource by setting aside a small portion of your income regularly. Consider automating your savings to make the process easier and more consistent. Additionally, keep these funds in a separate, easily accessible account to avoid the temptation of using them for non-emergencies.

In summary, while focusing on the long-term vision of a secure retirement is essential, take notice of the short-term necessity of an emergency fund. This financial safety net is vital to protecting your retirement savings, ensuring that when life throws you a financial challenge, you're well-prepared to face it head-on without derailing your plans.

Legal Documents to Protect Your Assets

As you diligently save for retirement, it's equally essential to safeguard your assets. While an emergency fund is a critical buffer for unexpected expenses, legal documents are the bedrock for protecting your assets and ensuring they are managed according to your wishes, both during your lifetime and after.

A will is one of the most fundamental documents in your asset protection arsenal. A will is a legal declaration by which you, the testator, name one or more persons to manage your estate and provide for the transfer of your property at death. Without a will, the state decides how your assets are distributed, which may not align with your wishes. By creating a will, you can dictate who inherits your assets, from your retirement accounts to your family heirlooms.

Another key document is a durable power of attorney. This allows you to appoint a trusted individual to manage your affairs if incapacitated. It's a common misconception that your spouse or adult children can automatically step in to make decisions on your behalf. In reality, with a power of attorney, they could petition the court to be named their guardian. This process can be time-consuming and stressful.

In addition to a power of attorney for financial matters, you should consider a healthcare power of attorney or proxy. This document appoints someone to make medical decisions on your behalf if you cannot do so. It's often paired with a living will, which outlines your wishes regarding life-sustaining treatment if you're terminally ill or permanently unconscious.

A trust might be a suitable option for those with more complex financial situations. Trusts come in various forms and can offer greater control over how your assets are distributed. For example, a revocable living trust allows you to retain control over the assets during your lifetime. It specifies how they should be handled after your death. Trusts can also help minimize estate taxes and offer protection from creditors and legal judgments.

Beneficiary designations are another critical component of protecting your retirement savings. These designations are typically found on life insurance policies, retirement accounts like 401(k)s and IRAs, and other financial accounts. Review and update these designations regularly, especially after significant life events like marriage, divorce, or the birth of a child, to ensure that your assets are passed on to the intended recipients.

Lastly, it's prudent to keep all these documents in a secure but accessible location and to inform your appointed representatives of their whereabouts. Regular reviews with a financial advisor or attorney can help ensure that your legal documents remain up-to-date with your current wishes and any changes in the law.

By taking these steps, you can rest assured that your retirement savings and other assets are protected. This provides you with peace of mind and simplifies the management of your estate for your loved ones, ensuring that your legacy is preserved according to your exact specifications.

Chapter Summary

- As retirees transition from work to retirement, they must reassess their insurance needs, as employer-provided coverage often ends.

- Health insurance is critical for retirees, especially those under 65 who aren't yet eligible for Medicare, and supplemental insurance may be needed even after Medicare eligibility.
- Long-term care insurance can protect retirement savings from the high long-term care costs, which Medicare does not typically cover.
- Life insurance needs may decrease if dependents no longer rely on the retiree's income. Still, it remains essential for those with dependents or debts.
- Liability insurance, such as an umbrella policy, can protect retirees from lawsuits threatening their savings.
- Regularly reviewing and adjusting insurance coverage is essential to meet changing needs throughout retirement.
- Working with a financial advisor or insurance professional can help retirees navigate complex insurance decisions and find the best coverage.
- Protecting retirement savings involves careful consideration of insurance needs to avoid unforeseen expenses and enjoy a more secure retirement.

8

NAVIGATING RETIREMENT CHALLENGES

Coping with Unexpected Life Events

Life is full of surprises; not all come with a bow. As you journey towards retirement, it's crucial to acknowledge that unexpected life events can and often do occur, potentially derailing even the most well-thought-out plans. Coping with these events is not just about having a contingency plan but cultivating resilience and adaptability in your financial strategy.

One of the most common unforeseen events is a health crisis. An accident or illness can lead to significant medical expenses that aren't fully covered by insurance, and it may also limit your ability to work temporarily or permanently. To mitigate this risk, consider purchasing comprehensive health insurance and exploring disability insurance options. Building and maintaining an emergency fund can also provide a financial buffer to help cover out-of-pocket expenses without dipping into your retirement savings.

Another unexpected event could be the loss of a job. Whether due to downsizing, company closure, or other reasons, the loss of steady income can be a significant setback. If you're nearing retirement, this might mean finding a new job or adjusting your retirement timeline. To prepare for such a scenario, try to diversify your income streams. This could involve part-time work, freelancing, or passive income sources like rental properties or investment dividends.

Family dynamics can also change unexpectedly and impact your retirement planning. For instance, you might find yourself in a situation where you need to support an adult child financially, or you may need to contribute to the care of aging parents. These responsibilities can strain your retirement savings if not planned for. To address this, consider setting clear boundaries on financial support and exploring insurance products like long-term care insurance for elderly relatives.

Lastly, divorce or losing a spouse can profoundly affect your retirement plans. Not only do these events have emotional ramifications, but they can also have financial consequences, such as the division of assets or loss of a second income. Reviewing and updating your retirement plan to reflect your new circumstances is essential, and seeking professional financial advice if needed.

In all cases, the key to coping with unexpected life events is flexibility. Regularly review and adjust your retirement plan to accommodate changes in your life. Keep informed about your financial situation. Feel free to seek advice from financial advisors who can provide personalized guidance tailored to your circumstances.

Remember, while you can't predict every twist and turn life throws at you, you can prepare to navigate through them with confidence and poise. By doing so, you'll protect your retirement savings and give yourself peace of mind, knowing you're as ready as you can be for whatever lies ahead.

Managing Inflation Impact on Retirement Savings

Inflation is often likened to a silent thief that can slowly erode the purchasing power of your hard-earned retirement savings. As you embark on the retirement planning journey, understanding and managing the impact of inflation is crucial. It's not just about how much you save but also how much those savings will be worth when you need them.

To begin with, it's essential to recognize that inflation is a normal part of economic life. Prices for goods and services rise over time, meaning that the dollar you save today will likely buy less. This is particularly important for retirees, who may be on fixed incomes and have less opportunity to increase their earnings.

One of the most effective strategies to counteract inflation is to include investments in your portfolio that can grow at a rate that outpaces inflation. Historically, equities or stocks have provided returns that exceed inflation over the long term. However, they come with higher volatility and risk. Including a diversified mix of stocks in your retirement portfolio can help maintain the purchasing power of your savings.

Another approach is to consider Treasury Inflation-Protected Securities (TIPS). TIPS are government bonds specifically designed to protect against inflation. The principal value of TIPS rises with inflation and falls with deflation, which can provide a measure of security in a fluctuating economy.

It's also wise to gradually increase your withdrawal rate to account for rising costs. A common rule of thumb is the 4% rule, which suggests withdrawing 4% of your retirement savings in the first year and then adjusting that amount for inflation each subsequent year. However, this rule is not one-size-fits-all, and you may need to tailor your withdrawal strategy based on your circumstances and market conditions.

In addition to investment strategies, staying flexible with your spending can be a powerful tool. This might mean adjusting your budget to prioritize essential expenses and finding ways to reduce costs or increase efficiency in your day-to-day life. For example, downsizing your home, using public transportation, or taking advantage of senior discounts can all help stretch your retirement dollars further.

Lastly, consider working with a financial advisor who can help you navigate the complexities of inflation and retirement planning. A professional can provide personalized advice and help you adjust your plan to address the changing economic landscape.

By taking proactive steps to manage the impact of inflation, you can better ensure that your retirement savings will support you throughout your golden years. Remember, the goal is not just to save but to maintain the value of those savings so you can enjoy the retirement you've worked so hard to achieve.

Adjusting Your Plan for Market Volatility

Market volatility can be a daunting aspect of retirement planning. The ups and downs of the stock market can significantly affect the value of your retirement savings, primarily if you are heavily invested in equities. However, with a few strategic adjustments to your retirement plan, you can navigate these choppy waters and maintain a course toward a secure retirement.

Firstly, it's essential to understand that market volatility is expected in investing. While it can be unsettling to see the value of your investments fluctuate, remember that retirement planning is a long-term endeavor. Over time, markets have historically trended upward despite short-term fluctuations.

One of the most effective strategies for dealing with market volatility is diversification. By spreading your investments across different asset classes, such as stocks, bonds, and real estate, you can reduce the risk that a downturn in any area will devastate your overall portfolio. Diversification can provide a buffer against the unpredictable nature of the markets.

Another key tactic is to have a well-thought-out asset allocation strategy that aligns with your risk tolerance and retirement timeline. As you approach retirement, it's generally advisable to gradually shift your asset allocation to include more conservative investments, like bonds, which are less susceptible to market swings. This can help protect the money you'll need to access in the near term.

Rebalancing your portfolio periodically is also crucial. This involves selling some investments that have increased in value and buying others that have decreased to maintain your desired asset allocation. Rebalancing helps you stick to your investment strategy. It can prevent you from being overly exposed to risk during market highs or lows.

An often-overlooked aspect of adjusting for market volatility is maintaining an emergency fund. Having a cash reserve can be particularly helpful during market stress, as it allows you to cover your living expenses without selling investments at a loss.

Lastly, it's important not to let emotions drive your investment decisions. Making impulsive choices during a market downturn can lock in losses and derail your retirement plan. Instead, focus on your long-term goals and consult a financial advisor to help guide you through turbulent times.

By implementing these strategies, you can create a retirement plan that is better equipped to handle the inevitable market volatility. This will allow you to focus on what truly matters: enjoying your retirement years with peace of mind, knowing you have a plan to adapt to changing financial landscapes.

Dealing with the Loss of a Spouse

The loss of a spouse is a profound event that can shake the very foundations of your life, not least of which is your financial stability and retirement planning. It's a time of deep emotional distress, and the added pressure of financial decisions can feel overwhelming. However, navigating this difficult period with care can help ensure that you remain on a stable financial path for the years to come.

First and foremost, permit yourself to grieve. Acknowledging your emotions and seeking support from friends, family, or a professional counselor is vital. Financial decisions can wait during the initial period of mourning.

Once you're ready to focus on practical matters, taking stock of your current financial situation is crucial. This includes understanding the full scope of your assets, liabilities, and income streams. You'll need to review all accounts, including bank accounts, retirement accounts, investment portfolios, and insurance policies. It's also essential to update any beneficiary designations that may have been in your spouse's name.

Social Security benefits will also need to be addressed. You might be eligible for survivor benefits if your spouse was receiving benefits. The rules surrounding these benefits can be complex, so consider consulting with a Social Security Administration representative or a financial advisor who can guide you through the process.

Adjusting your budget is another critical step. Your household expenses may have changed, and you must create a new budget that reflects your current income and expenses. This may also be an excellent time to reevaluate your retirement goals and timelines.

You may need to work a few more years than initially planned or decide to downsize your home to reduce living expenses.

Estate settlement is another area that will require attention. You'll need to locate your spouse's will and any other estate planning documents, such as trusts, and begin settling the estate. This can be a complex task, and it's often wise to enlist the help of an estate attorney to navigate the legalities and ensure that your spouse's wishes are honored.

Lastly, it's essential to review and update your estate plan. This includes your will, powers of attorney, and health care directives. It's a step that protects your assets and provides clarity and direction for your loved ones in the event of your own passing.

In dealing with the loss of a spouse, remember that you don't have to make all these decisions alone. Lean on trusted family members, friends, and professionals who can offer support and guidance. By taking measured steps, you can regain control of your financial life and continue confidently moving forward into retirement.

As you stabilize your financial footing after such a significant life change, it's also essential to consider the broader context of your retirement, including the dynamics within your family. Open communication about expectations, responsibilities, and support can ensure that your retirement years are as fulfilling and stress-free as possible.

Family Dynamics and Retirement

As we gracefully accept the changes that come with losing a spouse, we must also focus on the broader family dynamics that play a pivotal role in retirement. The family unit, often a source of support and comfort, can also present unique challenges during this phase of life. Understanding and navigating these relationships is crucial for a fulfilling retirement.

Firstly, the concept of dependency can shift significantly during retirement. If you have children, they may have reached adulthood and independence, which can alter your role within the family. This change can affect your sense of purpose and require adjusting how you interact with your children. It's essential to foster a balance between offering guidance and allowing them the freedom to make their own decisions. Additionally, the arrival of grandchildren can bring joy and new responsibilities, potentially impacting your retirement plans.

Secondly, your retirement can also affect your relationship with your siblings and extended family. You may find yourself able to care for aging relatives or support siblings going through their own life transitions. These responsibilities can be rewarding but can also add complexity to your retirement planning. Communicating openly with family members about your capacity to provide support while maintaining your well-being is essential.

Another aspect to consider is your potential financial support to family members. Whether helping a child with a down payment on a house, contributing to a grandchild's education, or assisting a sibling in need, these decisions can have significant implications for your retirement savings. It's essential to evaluate your financial situation and set clear boundaries to ensure that your generosity does not compromise your financial security.

Moreover, retirement can sometimes lead to increased time spent with family, which can be both a blessing and a source of stress. Differences in opinions, lifestyles, and values can emerge during extended family gatherings. It's beneficial to approach these situations with patience and understanding and to seek common ground that strengthens family bonds.

Finally, it's worth acknowledging that some retirees may face the challenge of feeling disconnected from family. Whether due to geographical distance, strained relationships, or the pursuit of different interests, finding ways to stay connected is essential. This could involve regular communication through phone calls, video chats, or planning family reunions. Engaging in shared activities or hobbies can also provide opportunities to create new memories and reinforce family ties.

In conclusion, retirement is not just a personal journey but one that intertwines with the lives of those we hold dear. You can navigate these challenges successfully by approaching family dynamics with empathy, clear communication, and a willingness to adapt. Remember, the goal is to build a retirement that is financially secure and rich in the relationships that matter most.

Chapter Summary

- Acknowledge that unexpected life events can affect retirement plans and cultivate financial resilience and adaptability.
- Prepare for health crises with comprehensive health insurance, disability insurance, and an emergency fund.
- Diversify income streams to mitigate the impact of job loss and consider part-time work or passive income sources.
- Plan for changes in family dynamics, such as supporting adult children or aging parents, and set financial boundaries.
- Update retirement plans after divorce or loss of a spouse and seek professional financial advice if necessary.
- Counteract inflation by investing in assets that outpace inflation, like equities and Treasury Inflation-Protected Securities (TIPS).
- Adjust for market volatility by diversifying investments, rebalancing portfolios, and maintaining an emergency fund.
- Navigate the loss of a spouse by allowing time to grieve, understand finances, adjust budgets, and update estate plans.

9

ESTATE PLANNING AND LEGACY

The Essentials of Estate Planning

As you embark on the retirement planning journey, it's crucial to understand that preparing for the future isn't just about ensuring you have enough money to live on. It's also about ensuring your assets and legacy are handled according to your wishes after you're gone. This is where estate planning comes into play, serving as a critical component of a comprehensive retirement plan.

Estate planning, at its core, is about control and care. It's legally structuring the future disposition of current and projected assets. It's not just for the wealthy; everyone has an estate, the total of all their assets, and everyone can benefit from a well-thought-out plan.

The first step in estate planning is taking stock of what you own. This includes tangible assets like your home, car, and personal possessions and intangible assets such as investments, insurance policies, and business interests. Once you have a clear picture of your assets, consider how you want them distributed.

One of the most straightforward tools in estate planning is the will. A will is a legal document that outlines how you want your property and assets to be distributed after your death. It can also specify guardians for any minor children. Without a will, the state decides how to distribute your assets, which may not align with your wishes.

However, a will is just one part of the estate planning process. Other components can include powers of attorney, allowing you to appoint someone to make decisions on your behalf if you cannot. There are two main types: a healthcare power of attorney, which covers medical decisions, and a financial power of attorney, which covers financial and legal decisions.

Another important aspect of estate planning is the designation of beneficiaries on accounts such as life insurance policies, retirement accounts, and bank accounts. These designations often override instructions in a will, so keeping them updated and in line with your estate planning goals is essential.

Trusts can be a valuable tool for those with more complex estates or specific wishes. Trusts come in various forms and can offer benefits such as avoiding probate, reducing estate taxes, and protecting assets from creditors.

Estate planning also involves considering the potential tax implications of inheritance. While not everyone's estate will be subject to estate taxes, it's essential to understand how these taxes work and what can be done to minimize them.

Lastly, reviewing and updating your estate plan regularly is vital, especially after significant life events like marriage, divorce, the birth of a child, or the acquisition of significant assets. An outdated estate plan can create confusion and conflict among your heirs. It may not reflect your current wishes or financial situation.

Remember, estate planning is a personal process and can be as simple or complex as your situation requires. It's about preserving your legacy and caring for your loved ones in the way you intend. With careful planning and the help of professionals like attorneys and financial advisors, you can create an estate plan that provides peace of mind for you and your family.

Wills and Trusts: Understanding the Basics

It's crucial to understand the foundational elements that ensure your legacy is preserved and your wishes are honored. Two elements are **wills** and **trusts**, each playing a distinct role in orchestrating your estate's future.

A will, often called a last will, is a legal document articulating your desires regarding the distribution of your assets and the care of any minor children upon your passing. It's the most basic estate planning tool, and it's essential for anyone looking to have a say in how their estate is handled after death. Without a will, the state's intestacy laws take over, and these may not align with your wishes.

Creating a will is a straightforward process requiring careful attention to detail. You'll need to appoint an executor, the person responsible for carrying out the instructions in your will. Choosing someone trustworthy and capable of managing the role's responsibilities is essential. You'll also need to be clear about who receives what, whether it's a family heirloom, a sum of money, or a piece of real estate. Being specific in your will can help prevent disputes among your heirs and ensure that your assets are distributed according to your wishes.

On the other hand, trusts are slightly more complex but offer additional benefits that a will alone cannot provide. A trust is a fiduciary arrangement allowing a third party, or trustee, to hold assets on behalf of a beneficiary or beneficiary. Trusts can be arranged in many ways and specify how and when the assets pass to the beneficiaries. Unlike wills, trusts typically avoid probate, the legal process through which a will is validated. This means that the distribution of assets can occur more quickly, privately, and often with fewer expenses and taxes.

There are various types of trusts designed to address different estate planning goals. For instance, a revocable living trust allows you to maintain control over the trust assets during your lifetime. It provides for transferring those assets after death, all while avoiding probate. An irrevocable trust, once established, generally cannot be altered, but it can offer significant tax benefits and asset protection.

When considering whether a will or a trust is more appropriate for your situation, evaluating the size and complexity of your estate, your privacy preferences, and your long-term objectives is essential. For many, combining a will and a trust is the most effective way to ensure comprehensive estate planning.

Remember, estate planning is not a one-size-fits-all process. It's a deeply personal journey that reflects your unique circumstances, values, and aspirations. As you contemplate the creation of a will or trust, it's wise to consult with an estate planning attorney who can guide you through the nuances of each option and help you craft a plan that aligns with your vision for the future.

With a solid understanding of wills and trusts, you're better equipped to make informed decisions about structuring your estate plan. This knowledge is a stepping stone to the next aspect of estate planning: designating beneficiaries for your assets and ensuring that your legacy is passed on according to your wishes.

Beneficiary Designations and Their Importance

As we delve into the intricacies of estate planning, it's crucial to understand the role of beneficiary designations and why they are a cornerstone of a well-structured retirement plan. While wills and trusts are essential for outlining your wishes, beneficiary designations are direct and often expedited means of transferring assets upon passing.

Beneficiary designations are unique in bypassing the probate process, the legal procedure through which a will is validated. This means that assets like life insurance policies, retirement accounts, and annuities can be transferred swiftly and directly to the individuals you've named without the potential delays and public scrutiny that come with probate.

One of the first steps in ensuring your beneficiary designations are in order is to take stock of all your accounts, allowing such designations. These typically include your 401(k), IRA, pension plans, life insurance policies, and any other accounts with payable-on-death (POD) or transfer-on-death (TOD) features. It's a common misconception that your will has the final say over these assets. Still, the named beneficiary on each account will take precedence.

The importance of keeping your beneficiary designations current cannot be overstated. Life events such as marriage, divorce, the birth of a child, or the death of a loved one can significantly alter your intentions for your legacy. Failing to update your designations to reflect these changes can lead to unintended consequences, such as an ex-spouse receiving benefits or a newborn child being unintentionally excluded.

When selecting beneficiaries, you have the option to name primary and contingent beneficiaries. The primary beneficiary is your first choice to receive the asset. In contrast, the contingent beneficiary is your alternate choice if the primary beneficiary predeceases you or cannot inherit for any reason. This layered approach adds extra security to ensure that your assets are distributed according to your wishes.

It's also possible to name multiple beneficiaries for a single account and to specify the proportions each should receive. This can be a helpful way to divide assets among children or other heirs. However, your designations must be clear and precise to ensure clarity and clarity among your beneficiaries.

In addition to individuals, you can name trusts as beneficiaries, which can be particularly advantageous if you wish to provide for minors or individuals with special needs or if you want to impose certain conditions on the inheritance. However, this requires careful coordination with your overall estate plan to ensure that the trust's terms align with your goals and are appropriately structured to receive the designated assets.

Lastly, reviewing your beneficiary designations periodically is advisable as part of an annual financial review or whenever significant life changes occur. This practice ensures that your estate plan aligns with your current circumstances and intentions.

In summary, beneficiary designations are a powerful tool in retirement planning, offering a direct and efficient way to pass on your legacy. By thoughtfully selecting and routinely updating your beneficiaries, you can ensure that your assets are distributed according to your wishes, providing peace of mind for you and your loved ones.

Charitable Giving and Philanthropy

As you approach retirement, you've likely considered how to manage your assets and ensure they provide for your loved ones. But another aspect of estate planning can be equally fulfilling: charitable giving and philanthropy. This is not just the preserve of the ultra-wealthy; anyone can leave a philanthropic legacy that reflects their values and supports the causes they care about.

Charitable giving as part of your estate plan can take many

forms, and it's essential to understand your options. One of the simplest ways to include charity in your estate plan is through a bequest in your will. You can specify a certain amount of money, a percentage of your estate, or particular assets to go to a charity of your choice. This is a straightforward way to make a significant impact, often without affecting your finances during your lifetime.

Another option is to name a charity as a beneficiary of your retirement accounts or life insurance policies. This can be an efficient way to give, as the assets typically transfer directly to the charity without going through probate. It can also have tax advantages, as the charity is tax-exempt, and the money will not be considered part of your taxable estate.

For those who wish to see their philanthropic efforts take effect during their lifetime, establishing a charitable trust might be the right choice. There are several types of charitable trusts, but they all allow you to contribute assets to a trust that will eventually benefit your chosen charity. Some, like a charitable remainder trust, can provide you or other named beneficiaries with income for some time before the remaining assets go to the charity.

Donor-advised funds (DAFs) are another popular vehicle for charitable giving. A DAF allows you to make a charitable contribution, receive an immediate tax deduction, and then recommend grants from the fund to your preferred charities over time. This can be an excellent way to involve family members in philanthropy and to create a lasting family legacy of giving.

It's also worth considering the potential tax benefits of charitable giving as part of your estate plan. Depending on how you structure your giving, you may reduce estate taxes, income taxes, or both. For example, assets given to charity are generally not subject to estate taxes, and contributions to charitable trusts or donor-advised funds may provide income tax deductions.

When incorporating charitable giving into your estate plan, working with an experienced estate planning attorney and possibly a financial advisor is crucial. They can help you understand the implications of different giving strategies and ensure that your philanthropic goals are met in a way that complements your overall estate plan.

Remember, philanthropy is deeply personal. Your charitable giving should reflect the causes and organizations you are passionate about. By thoughtfully integrating charitable strategies into your estate planning, you can create a legacy that extends beyond your lifetime and makes a lasting difference in the world.

Transferring Wealth to the Next Generation

As you approach the later stages of life, it's natural to start thinking about the legacy you'll leave behind. For many, this includes ensuring that the wealth they've accumulated over the years is passed on to the next generation in a manner that is both efficient and reflective of their wishes. Transferring wealth is not just a matter of handing over assets; it's a process that requires thoughtful planning and consideration of both financial and emotional implications.

One of the first steps in transferring wealth to your heirs is to understand what you own clearly. This includes tangible assets like property and personal belongings and intangible assets such as investments and retirement accounts. Once you have a comprehensive inventory, you must consider how each asset should be distributed. This is where a will becomes an essential tool. A will is a legal document that outlines your wishes regarding the distribution of your assets and the care of any minor children after your death.

However, a will is just one part of a larger estate plan. You'll need to designate beneficiaries for many assets, such as life insurance policies and retirement accounts. These designations are powerful, often superseding instructions in a will, so keeping them up to date and in line with your current wishes is essential.

Trusts are another critical element of estate planning that can provide greater control over how your assets are distributed. A trust can help minimize estate taxes, protect assets from creditors, and ensure that your wealth is managed according to your directives. There are various types of trusts, each with specific advantages, and choosing the right one depends on your circumstances and goals.

Taxes are an inevitable part of transferring wealth, and it's crucial to understand their impact on your estate. Estate, inheritance, and income taxes can diminish the value of the assets you leave behind if not properly managed. Working with a financial advisor or estate planner can help you develop strategies to minimize these taxes and preserve more of your wealth for your heirs.

It's also essential to have open conversations with your beneficiaries about your estate plan. Discussing your intentions can help prevent misunderstandings and conflicts after you're gone. It's an opportunity to explain your decisions, share your values, and set expectations. These conversations can be difficult but essential for a smooth wealth transition.

Finally, remember that estate planning is not a one-time task. Your life circumstances and the laws governing estate planning can change, so reviewing and updating your plan regularly is essential. This ensures that your estate plan continues to align with your current situation and that your legacy is preserved as you intend.

By taking these steps, you can create a thoughtful and effective plan for transferring wealth to the next generation, ensuring that your legacy is carried on in the way you envision.

Chapter Summary

- Estate planning is essential for controlling the distribution of assets and ensuring one's legacy is honored after death.

- It involves cataloging assets, creating a will, setting up powers of attorney, and designating beneficiaries.
- Trusts can be used for more complex estates to avoid probate, reduce taxes, and protect assets.
- Regularly updating the estate plan is crucial, especially after significant life events.
- Wills and trusts are fundamental tools in estate planning, with trusts offering benefits like avoiding probate.
- Beneficiary designations on accounts like life insurance and retirement plans are crucial as they supersede wills.
- Charitable giving can be incorporated into estate plans through bequests, trusts, or donor-advised funds, offering potential tax benefits.
- Transferring wealth to the next generation requires a precise inventory of assets, an understanding of tax implications, and open communication with heirs.

10

STAYING FINANCIALLY FIT IN RETIREMENT

Reviewing and Adjusting Your Financial Plan

Embarking on retirement is akin to setting sail on a long-anticipated voyage. You've charted your course and stocked up on provisions, and now it's time to navigate the open waters of your golden years. But just as the sea is ever-changing, so is the financial landscape of retirement. To ensure that you remain financially fit throughout this journey, reviewing and adjusting your financial plan periodically is essential.

Think of your financial plan as a living document that requires regular attention and tweaking. Life throws curveballs, and your financial strategy needs to be flexible enough to catch them. Whether it's a change in health, unexpected expenses, or shifts in the economy, your plan should be robust enough to accommodate these changes.

Start by revisiting your budget. Retirement often brings about a shift in spending patterns. Perhaps you're traveling more or have taken up new hobbies that require additional funding. Conversely, some of your anticipated expenses are lower than expected. Review your income streams and expenses at least once a year to ensure they align with your retirement goals.

Next, consider the performance of your investments. The financial markets can be volatile, and the appropriate asset allocation when you first retire might not be suitable a few years later. It's wise to assess your investment portfolio regularly with a critical eye. Are your investments providing the returns you need? Are they too risky or not risky enough? Adjustments may be necessary to strike the right balance between growth and preservation of capital.

Inflation is another factor that can erode your purchasing power over time. Your financial plan should account for a gradual increase in the cost of living. This might mean shifting some of your assets into investments that have the potential to outpace inflation, such as stocks or real estate while maintaining a portion in more stable investments like bonds or certificates of deposit for security.

Remember to review your estate plan as well. Changes in your family situation, such as marriages, divorces, births, or deaths, can have significant implications for your estate. Ensure that your will, powers of attorney, and beneficiary designations are up to date and reflect your current wishes.

Lastly, it's crucial to monitor tax laws, which can change and impact your retirement savings and income. Tax-efficient withdrawal strategies can help you keep more of your hard-earned money. Consult with a tax professional to understand the latest tax regulations and take advantage of any new tax-saving opportunities.

By regularly reviewing and adjusting your financial plan, you can stay ahead of retirement's changes. This proactive approach allows you to maintain financial fitness, ensuring that your retirement savings last as long as you do and that you can enjoy the retirement lifestyle you've worked so hard to achieve.

The Role of a Financial Advisor

As you embark on the retirement journey, one of the most significant transitions involves shifting from accumulating wealth to managing and preserving it. This is where the expertise of a financial advisor can become invaluable. A financial advisor is not just a guide; they are your partner in maintaining financial health throughout retirement.

Financial advisors bring a wealth of knowledge in investment strategies, tax laws, and estate planning, which can be complex and ever-changing. They help you navigate these waters, ensuring your retirement savings are optimized for growth and sustainability.

One of the primary responsibilities of a financial advisor is to assess your current financial situation and develop a plan that aligns with your retirement goals. This includes evaluating your income sources, such as Social Security, pensions, and investment accounts, and crafting a strategy that addresses your desired lifestyle and any unforeseen expenses.

A financial advisor will also assist in creating a withdrawal strategy that minimizes tax liabilities and maximizes the longevity of your savings. They can help determine which accounts to draw from first and how to adjust your withdrawals in response to market fluctuations and personal circumstances.

Moreover, a financial advisor can offer guidance on handling healthcare costs, often representing a significant portion of retirement expenses. They can suggest insurance options and planning techniques to protect your assets from potential long-term care costs.

Another critical aspect of a financial advisor's role is to provide a buffer against emotional decision-making. The ups and downs of the market can prompt retirees to make hasty choices that might jeopardize their financial well-being. A financial advisor offers an objective perspective, helping you stick to your long-term plan and adjust as needed without reacting to short-term market movements.

In addition to helping with financial decisions, a good financial advisor will also educate you about your investments and the rationale behind each recommendation. This empowers you to make informed decisions and fosters a sense of confidence and control over your financial future.

Lastly, a financial advisor ensures that your financial plan stays current. Life events, such as the loss of a spouse, moving to a new home, or even changes in the tax code, can all necessitate a review and potential adjustment of your financial strategy. Your advisor will be there to help you through these changes, providing the necessary advice to keep your retirement plan on track.

In summary, a financial advisor plays a multifaceted role in helping you stay financially fit in retirement. They are not only planners and strategists but also educators and confidants. With their expertise, you can feel more secure in your financial future, knowing that you have a professional looking out for your best interests as you enjoy your retirement.

Staying Informed on Economic Changes

As you transition from the working world into retirement, it's crucial to understand that staying financially fit doesn't just involve managing your savings and investments. It also requires keeping a keen eye on the broader economic landscape. The economy is dynamic and constantly in flux due to many factors, including interest rates, inflation, market trends, and global events. These changes can significantly impact your retirement funds, and being informed can help you navigate potential financial challenges.

Firstly, it's essential to recognize that economic changes can affect the purchasing power of your retirement savings. Inflation, for instance, can erode the value of money over time, meaning that what you can buy with a dollar today may differ five or ten years later. To mitigate this, you should consider investments that have the potential to outpace inflation, such as stocks or real estate, while also maintaining a portion of your portfolio in more stable assets for protection against market volatility.

Another aspect to consider is interest rates, which can influence the returns on fixed-income investments like bonds. When interest rates rise, the value of existing bonds typically falls since new bonds may be issued at higher rates, making them more attractive to investors. Conversely, when interest rates fall, existing bonds with higher rates become more valuable. Understanding these relationships can help you make more informed decisions about structuring your investment portfolio.

Keeping abreast of economic changes also means paying attention to tax laws, which can directly affect your retirement savings. Tax laws are subject to change, and new legislation can alter the landscape of retirement planning. For example, changes in tax rates or rules governing retirement account withdrawals can impact your financial strategy. Staying informed through reputable financial news sources, professional financial advisors, or educational seminars can help you anticipate and adjust to these changes.

Moreover, global economic events, such as international trade agreements or geopolitical conflicts, can also influence the markets. Diversifying your investments internationally can help spread risk and offer growth opportunities not tied to a single country's economic conditions.

In essence, staying informed on economic changes is not about reacting to every news headline or market swing. Instead, it's about solidifying how these changes can affect your retirement strategy and being prepared to make adjustments when necessary. This proactive approach can help you maintain financial fitness throughout your retirement years, ensuring your golden years remain as secure and enjoyable as possible.

Remember, the goal is not to become a financial expert overnight but to stay sufficiently informed to make wise decisions and consult with your financial advisor when needed. This approach will set the stage for continued learning and financial education, a critical component of managing your finances in retirement.

Continued Learning and Financial Education

It's crucial to understand that financial education is not a one-time event but a lifelong journey as you transition into retirement. With the basics of economic changes under your belt, it's time to focus on the importance of continued learning and financial education to stay financially fit during retirement.

Firstly, consider the financial landscape as a constantly evolving ecosystem. Just as professionals must keep up with developments in their fields, retirees should stay abreast of the latest trends in personal finance, tax laws, and investment strategies. You can still become a financial expert, but having a solid understanding of the basics can help you make informed decisions that align with your retirement goals.

One effective way to continue your financial education is by seeking out resources designed for retirees. Many community colleges and adult education programs offer retirement planning, estate planning, and investment management courses. These classes can provide valuable insights into the complexities of retirement finances and offer strategies for managing your money effectively.

Additionally, many books, online courses, and websites are dedicated to personal finance and retirement planning. Look for materials that break down complex financial concepts into digestible information. Remember, the goal is to empower yourself with knowledge, not to overwhelm yourself with jargon and intricacies best left to professionals.

Speaking of professionals, periodically consulting with a financial advisor can also be part of your continued learning. A good advisor can help you understand your current financial situation, adjust your investment portfolio as needed, and plan for future expenses. They can also serve as a sounding board for any financial ideas or concerns you may have.

Another critical aspect of continued learning is staying connected with your peers. Joining retirement groups or online forums can be an excellent way to share experiences and learn from others navigating similar financial waters. These communities often discuss managing retirement income, dealing with healthcare costs, and maximizing social security benefits.

Lastly, make it a habit to review your financial plan regularly. Your financial plan should evolve as you learn more and your circumstances change. This could mean adjusting your budget, reevaluating your risk tolerance, or exploring new investment opportunities. You can adapt to changes and maintain a comfortable lifestyle throughout retirement by staying educated and proactive about your finances.

Remember, financial fitness in retirement is not a destination but a continuous process. By committing to ongoing education and staying curious about financial matters, you can enhance your financial savvy and enjoy the peace of mind that comes with being in control of your retirement destiny.

Embracing Technology for Financial Management

In the golden years of retirement, staying financially fit isn't just about what you've saved; it's also about how you manage and monitor those savings. As we continue our journey through the essentials of retirement planning, it's time to explore technology's role in keeping your finances in top shape.

Today, technology offers many tools that can simplify financial management, making it more efficient and often more secure. Embracing these technological solutions can help you keep a close eye on your retirement funds, track spending, and stay informed about the health of your investments.

Firstly, consider the convenience of online banking. Most financial institutions now provide secure online access to your accounts, allowing you to view balances, transfer funds, and pay bills from home. This saves time and reduces the need to physically visit a bank, which can be particularly advantageous if mobility becomes an issue.

Investment tracking apps are another boon for the tech-savvy retiree. These apps can aggregate information from various investment accounts, giving you a comprehensive view of your portfolio's performance. You can monitor the ups and downs of the market, assess the balance of your asset allocation, and make informed decisions about when to buy or sell.

Budgeting software is also a critical component of financial management in retirement. These programs can help you create a budget that aligns with your fixed income, track your spending, and even forecast future expenses. By closely monitoring where your money is going, you can ensure that you're living within your means and adjust your spending habits as necessary.

For those concerned about security, technology has made great strides in protecting your financial data. Two-factor authentication, biometric logins, and encryption are security features that can help safeguard your information. It's essential to use these features where available and to stay informed about best practices for online security.

Moreover, the rise of robo-advisors has made investment advice more accessible and affordable. These automated platforms use algorithms to provide personalized investment advice based on your financial goals and risk tolerance. For retirees needing more desire or means to hire a personal financial advisor, robo-advisors can be a valuable resource for maintaining a healthy investment strategy.

Lastly, pay attention to the educational resources available online. Countless websites, webinars, and online courses can help you stay informed about financial topics relevant to retirees. Whether you want to understand the tax implications of your retirement accounts or learn about new investment opportunities, the internet is a treasure trove of information.

In conclusion, technology can be a powerful ally in managing your retirement finances. By leveraging online banking, investment tracking apps, budgeting software, and educational resources, you can clearly understand your financial health and react swiftly to any changes. Remember, staying financially fit isn't a one-time effort; it's an ongoing process that benefits greatly from modern technology's tools and conveniences.

Chapter Summary

- Regularly review and adjust your financial plan for life changes and economic shifts.

- Revisit your budget annually to align with retirement goals, considering changes in spending and income.
- Assess investment performance and adjust asset allocation to balance growth and capital preservation.
- Plan for inflation by investing in assets that can outpace it while keeping stable investments for security.
- Update your estate plan for family changes and ensure all legal documents reflect current wishes.
- Stay informed on tax laws to optimize retirement savings and income, possibly consulting a tax professional.
- A financial advisor can help manage wealth, develop tax-efficient withdrawal strategies, and provide objective advice.
- Embrace technology for efficient financial management, using online banking, investment apps, budgeting software, and staying informed through online resources.

THE GOLDEN YEARS

Lessons Learned and Wisdom Gained

As we draw the curtains on this guide to retirement planning for beginners, it's essential to pause and distill the essence of what we've learned through our exploration. The journey to retirement is as unique as the individual embarking upon it. Yet, certain universal truths have emerged that can guide us toward a fulfilling and secure retirement.

Firstly, the importance of starting early must be considered. Time is a powerful ally in compounding interest and investment growth. Those who begin their retirement savings journey when they enter the workforce, even with modest amounts, often find themselves in a much more comfortable position later in life. It's a lesson in patience and foresight—attributes that serve well beyond financial planning.

Secondly, we've learned that knowledge is a form of wealth. Understanding the basics of financial instruments, the impact of taxes, and the benefits of various retirement accounts empowers you to make informed decisions. This education should be ongoing; the financial landscape is ever-changing, and staying informed is crucial to adapt your plan to new laws, products, and economic climates.

Another lesson is the significance of living within one's means. It's a simple concept, yet it's often challenging to practice consistently. Avoiding unnecessary debt, making prudent spending choices, and prioritizing savings are habits that build a solid financial foundation, ensuring that when retirement comes, it's a time of enjoyment rather than stress.

Diversification has also emerged as a critical strategy. Putting all your eggs in one basket can be a risky endeavor. By spreading investments across different asset classes, sectors, and even geographical regions, you can mitigate risk and increase the chances of steady growth over time.

Furthermore, we've seen the value of setting clear goals and revisiting them regularly. Retirement planning isn't a set-it-and-forget-it affair. Life's milestones—marriage, children, home purchases, and career changes—can all affect your retirement goals and strategies. Regularly assessing your plan ensures it remains aligned with your evolving life circumstances.

Lastly, the wisdom of seeking professional advice cannot be understated. While having a solid grasp of retirement planning fundamentals is essential, there's no substitute for personalized advice from a financial advisor. They can provide insights tailored to your situation, helping you navigate complex decisions and optimize your retirement plan.

As we move forward, let's carry these lessons with us. They are the building blocks for a retirement that's not only financially secure but also rich in the experiences and joys of having the freedom and peace of mind to enjoy your golden years truly.

The Importance of Flexibility and Adaptability

As we embrace the golden years of retirement, it's essential to understand that the journey is not only about the plans we've meticulously crafted but also about our ability to adapt to the unexpected twists and turns life may present. Flexibility and adaptability become critical components in ensuring that our retirement years are secure and fulfilling.

We often follow a structured path with clear goals and timelines throughout our working lives. However, retirement introduces a new level of freedom coupled with uncertainty. The stock market may fluctuate, health may change, and personal relationships may evolve—all factors impacting our retirement experience. It's here that being flexible with our plans and adaptable to change can make a significant difference.

Consider the financial aspect: a fixed-income portfolio that seemed perfect at the onset of retirement might need adjustments as economic conditions change. Being open to revisiting and revising your investment strategies can help safeguard your nest egg against inflation and market volatility. Similarly, healthcare needs often become more complex as we age. Staying informed about Medicare options and supplemental insurance plans and being willing to adjust coverage as health needs can prevent unexpected medical expenses from derailing your financial security.

On a more personal level, adaptability plays a crucial role in maintaining a vibrant social life and finding new passions. The activities and hobbies that excite you at the beginning of retirement may shift over time. Being open to exploring new interests, joining different community groups, or even relocating to a more retiree-friendly environment can enhance your quality of life.

Moreover, flexibility in your daily routine can lead to unexpected joys. You may discover a love for volunteering, mentoring, or part-time work in a field you've always been passionate about. These activities can structure your days while allowing you the freedom to set your own pace.

In essence, the golden years of retirement are not just a period to enjoy the fruits of your labor but also a time for growth and adaptation. By staying flexible in your plans and adaptable to the changing tides of life, you can navigate the uncertainties of retirement with confidence and grace. This approach ensures a more resilient financial standing and enriches your life with new experiences and opportunities for personal development.

As we move forward, the lessons we've learned and the wisdom we've gained become the legacy we pass on. It's not just about the assets we leave behind but also the example we set on how to live a whole and adaptable life in retirement.

Passing on Your Legacy

As you approach the twilight of your golden years, the concept of legacy becomes increasingly significant. Retirement planning is not just about ensuring you have the financial means to live comfortably; it's also about the mark you leave on the world and how you touch the lives of those you care about. Passing on your legacy is a multifaceted process that encompasses the tangible assets you've accumulated over a lifetime and the values, lessons, and memories you wish to bestow upon future generations.

Your legacy is the lasting impression you make, culminating in your life's work, beliefs, and the love you share. It's the stories your family recounts at gatherings, the wisdom you've imparted to your children and grandchildren, and your impact on your community. As you consider how you want to be remembered, consider how you can actively shape your legacy.

One practical step in passing on your legacy is to ensure your financial affairs are in order. This includes having an up-to-date will, considering trusts for asset protection, and making clear designations for beneficiaries on your financial accounts and insurance policies. It's also prudent to have conversations with your loved ones about your end-of-life wishes, including any medical directives or preferences for memorial services.

Beyond the financial aspect, consider writing a personal letter or recording a video message that shares your life stories, values, and hopes for your family's future. This can be an invaluable gift, providing comfort and guidance even when you're no longer physically present.

Engaging in philanthropy or charitable giving can also be a part of your legacy. Whether through regular donations, volunteering, or setting up a scholarship fund, these acts of kindness can carry your influence forward and reflect the causes you hold dear.

Remember, your legacy is not just about what you leave behind; it's also about how you live today. Continue to nurture relationships, invest in the growth of others, and contribute positively to your community. These actions will resonate and form the foundation of the legacy you pass on.

In the end, your legacy is a bridge between the past, present, and future. It's a way to ensure that your life's journey continues to inspire and guide those who follow in your footsteps. As you reflect on the legacy you wish to create, know it's always possible to make meaningful contributions that will echo through the generations.

Looking Ahead: Continuous Growth and Enjoyment

As we turn the page from considering the legacy we wish to leave behind, it's equally important to focus on our retirement years' present and future aspects. Retirement isn't a final destination; it's a new chapter that offers continuous growth and enjoyment. The key to a fulfilling retirement is to embrace this period as an opportunity for personal development and to find joy in the everyday.

Firstly, let's talk about growth. Retirement is the perfect time to explore interests you may have put on hold during your working years. Whether learning a new language, picking up a musical instrument, or diving into gardening, these activities are not just hobbies but avenues for mental stimulation and skill development. Lifelong learning keeps the mind sharp and can lead to a more satisfying retirement. Many community colleges and universities offer courses specifically designed for retirees, and online platforms provide endless opportunities to learn at your own pace.

In addition to intellectual growth, physical activity is paramount. Regular exercise can help manage health issues, improve mood, and increase social interaction. Joining a local walking group, signing up for dance classes, or simply dedicating time each day for a swim can significantly impact your overall well-being. Remember, it's not about intensity but consistency and finding an activity you enjoy.

Social engagement is another critical component of a rewarding retirement. Maintaining old friendships and building new ones can prevent feelings of isolation and provide a support network. Consider volunteer work, joining clubs, or participating in community events to stay connected with others. Social interactions can also provide a sense of purpose and belonging, which is essential for happiness at any age.

Financial health continues to be a priority, even after the initial stages of retirement planning. Reviewing your financial situation regularly is essential to ensure your savings and investments align with your current needs and future goals. This may involve adjusting your budget to accommodate changes in your lifestyle or consulting with a financial advisor to discuss any concerns.

Lastly, remember to savor the small moments that bring joy. Whether it's a morning cup of coffee on the porch, an afternoon spent with grandchildren, or an evening of stargazing, these simple pleasures can provide profound happiness. Retirement offers the luxury of time filled with the things that matter most to you.

In conclusion, your golden years can be just that—golden—if approached with a mindset geared towards continuous growth and enjoyment. By engaging in lifelong learning, staying physically active, maintaining social connections, managing your finances, and appreciating life's simple joys, you can craft a fulfilling and dynamic retirement. As we close this chapter on retirement planning, remember that your retirement story is one you continue to write daily with every choice and new adventure.

Your Feedback Matters

As we reach the end of this book, I extend my heartfelt gratitude for your time and engagement. It's been an honor to share this journey with you, and I hope it has been as enriching for you as it has been for me.

If the ideas we've explored have sparked new thoughts, inspired change, or provided comfort, I'd really appreciate it if you could share your experience with others. Your feedback benefits me as an author and guides fellow readers in their quest for their next meaningful read.

To leave a review on Amazon, follow the QR code below. Your insights and reflections are invaluable; by sharing them, you contribute to a larger conversation that extends far beyond the pages of this book.

Thank you once again for your company on this literary adventure. May the insights you've gained stay with you, and may your continuous quest for knowledge be ever-fulfilling.

SCAN ME

ABOUT THE AUTHOR

Calvin Boswell is a financial expert and author of the *"Financial Planning Essentials"* series, which simplifies retirement and estate planning for beginners. With over two decades of experience, he is known for his clear and accessible approach to personal finance, helping individuals confidently navigate their financial futures.

www.ingramcontent.com/pod-product-compliance
Lightning Source LLC
Chambersburg PA
CBHW071427210326
41597CB00020B/3680